Praise for Psychic Development Level 3

"The Anastasi System of Psychic Development Level 3, is part of one of the best psychic systems out there today as well as one of my personal favorites.

Sandy is able to take all that you have learned up to this point, and put it together with some of the divination tools and toys that many in the psychic field use. This class is not only fun, but it is also very educational. Sandy easily guides you through the steps to meet your spirit guides and helpers, as well as astral traveling. She then takes one step further and discusses ethics within the psychic field, something that everyone should utilize but is missed by many other systems.

Everything that Sandy teaches is done in an easy to understand and safe way that makes the student feel relaxed and comfortable. I highly suggest the Anastasi System of Psychic Development for anyone that may be interested in developing their abilities, or simply wanting to learn what it is all about.

Thank you Sandy, for bringing this vast knowledge to the public and in turn educating the world and helping so many people."

— Thomas Moore, High Priest, Intuitive Psychic

"Sandy, I have to say thank you for what you have done for me. Over the years of working with you and your psychic development classes you have been the best teacher and friend a person could have. You taught me to hone in on my skills and use them. Your skills as a psychic and a teacher are out of this world. You have done so much with your work and helping people just like me.

I am proud to call you my friend and teacher. Because of you Atlanta and surrounding areas are able to come here and learn the Anastasi System of Psychic Development. Thanks for all you've done and all you do."

— Carl Woodall

Books by Sandy Anastasi

The Anastasi System Psychic Development Series:

Level 1: The Fundamentals

Level 2: Energy and Auras

Level 3: Tools and Toys

Level 4: An Introduction to Channeling and Spirit Communication

Level 5: Developing the Energy and Skill in Spirit Communication

Level 6: Healing in Spirit Communication (to be released)

Astrology:

Astrology: Art and Science

Intermediate Astrology

Tarot:

Tarot Reader's Workbook: A Comprehensive Guide from Beginner to Master

Kabbala:

Pathworking the Kabbala

THE ANASTASI SYSTEM
PSYCHIC DEVELOPMENT SERIES

Level 3:
Tools and Toys
By Sandy Anastasi

Notices

The Anastasi System — Psychic Development Level 3: Tools and Toys

Notice of Rights:

Notice of Liability:

Acknowledgements

This work took thirty years to develop and has undergone countless revisions. During all this time I have been blessed by the support of some truly wonderful and special people. I want to take a moment to extend thanks to the following people, without whom it would never have come into existence: Ron Tourville, my husband, who has a way of making all things possible; John Maerz, who helped to develop and distribute the earliest versions of this book and series; my many students whose questions, interests and problems led me to refine and redefine the way the material was presented until I finally arrived at the present version. My good friend John Edward who has given his help and support in so many ways, not the least of which is through his own example; my family and friends for their belief, support and patience; Rick Rajter for his computer knowledge and excitement about the job; Emily Jack for her excellent proofreading and editing; and last but surely not least, Lisa Freeman, my personal assistant who has a knack for keeping track of it all... including me. You all have my deepest gratitude, and my love.

Table of Contents

Foreword

Paracelsus said, "Man has a natural light, but also a light outside the light of nature by which he can seek out supernatural things... and it should be known that when a man prophesies, he does not speak from the devil and not from the holy spirit, but from the innate spirit of the invisible body in which man has his origins."

As long as there have been people there have been psychics. People with a certain ability that has previously been loosely defined as intuitive in nature. Learning to develop those skills has, until now, been a nebulous process. With the advent of Sandy Anastasi's Psychic Development series no one must ever again bump around in the dark looking for a definitive, step-by-step process by which to learn and develop psychic abilities.

In addition to being Sandy's husband, I have the distinct pleasure of teaching this system with her. I was studying with another 'great' in the field of new age thought, Mary Alice Warren, when I realized my time with her had come to an end. As we spoke of this together, I asked if she would recommend someone with whom I could further my studies. Without hesitation she said, "Ron, you need to go see Sandy Anastasi."

Sandy has taken the mystery out of learning these practices with her down to earth approach and college-level curriculum. *Psychic Development Level 3: Tools and Toys* is my personal favorite. You will learn how to master the use of an array of tools, as well as learn to become more in touch with energy and the myriad of ways it affects us every day. I use this skill set in business with amazing results. In these pages are the words and exercises that can have a profound effect on how you see the world... Use them wisely!

So many others have rightly given Sandy's accomplishments first billing as they write about her, so allow me a line or two to give you some insight into the woman behind this series. There is a grace and calmness that is uniquely Sandy. We almost never hold a conversation where some piece of channeled information does not come forth. She LIVES this, she BREATHES this and it never ceases to amaze even her harshest critic that this course can take a rote beginner and help him to become proficient in his skills.

Blessings to you Sandy and to all of those who will benefit from your work.

The Reverend, Dr. Ronald Tourville

Author's Foreword

Psychic Development Level 3 was developed to give students who have worked with the meditations and exercises contained in Psychic Development Levels 1 and 2 additional tools through which they can apply their newly acquired abilities.

Originally, I introduced all of the tools contained in these pages immediately in Psychic Development Level 1. I found out very early on that most beginning level students had poor, if any, results using these tools without first studying, and to at least some degree mastering, the psychic development techniques taught in the earlier books. So, eventually I moved the tools to the third section of the Psychic Development series.

Now, I have great results with all of my students. These tools have really become toys. They are great fun to learn to work with. Most students will take a liking to one or two, and will usually incorporate them into their regular psychic readings. Just as with the psychic skills you have studied, you will tend to be better at certain things than others, although all the tools can be learned and all are fun.

Some of my students have asked why these tools are in the series at all. The answer is that they are an aid to psychic development, in many cases helping students to move to a new level of awareness. Also, in some cases when someone you are trying to read is particularly blocked or closed, tools such as the ones described in these pages can be a valuable aid in getting through the block so that you can do your psychic reading. Additionally, some of you reading these pages will find that you are much more confident in using your psychic abilities if they are backed up by a solid tool. Lastly, you will find that some of the people you do readings for feel much more confident in YOU if you are using a tool in conjunction with your straight psychic abilities of clairvoyance, telepathy, clairsentience, empathy, etc., that you developed when studying the skills discussed in the first two books of this series. Sometimes seeing something tangible like a pendulum or a crystal ball, or watching you hold something of the client's while you do *psychometry* gives your client a sense of security. There are also many instances where it is simply not possible to tune in without the aid of a tool such as I am going to show you how to use in these pages. For example, a psychic working to find a lost person often cannot link in strongly enough to the person unless they know how to psychometrize an object that belonged to the person, and use it as a link to him or her.

I will discuss many tools in great depth in these pages, giving you the ability to use them with confidence in your work. Exercises will be provided that help you to become not just proficient, but also excellent at using them. Other tools I'll just mention and describe, leaving you the option of pursuing them on your own. There are many resources other than this for the study all of these tools, and some of these that I feel are particularly effective will be mentioned as well.

Of course the protections that should be employed to safely open psychically to the use of each of these tools will also be provided. The use of some of these tools and techniques also requires a strong connection to both your Higher Self and your guides, so there will be many exercises designed to strengthen your connections to them, as well as to meet them.

As you learn to use each tool discussed you will also be learning something of its history and various ways it can be used. Wherever I can, I will give you direct examples from my own experience in using them. YOU will come to an understanding of their limitations and the benefits of using certain tools in specific instances. I will also do my best to tell you how to make the tools yourself or where to find them if they must be purchased.

I advise you to put the effort into practicing with all of the tools and techniques presented in these pages, and also to look into the additional ones mentioned, in order to fully investigate what areas you are particularly talented in. I cannot emphasize how much using and working with these various tools over the years has benefited me personally, as well as the clients I work with.

Introduction

Psychic Development Level 3 will teach you to do a variety of divination techniques using tools such as automatic writing, the crystal ball, the pendulum, psychometry, and astral travel. These are all easy to learn and use, and they are clearly presented with close attention paid to their safe practice. You will learn protections that will enable you to use all of these tools safely. Additionally, you will meet your Life Guide and your Protector Guide (whom some call their Guardian Angel) in these pages.

The tools you will learn in these pages are a wonderful help on the journey to develop your psychic ability. Many 'straight' psychics look down on the use of tools, believing that the reader who relies on them too much does not reach his or her full potential. The opposite is actually true. Using the tools you will encounter in these pages will help you to uncover and develop latent talents and will encourage you to spend more time on areas that, until now, were difficult for you. The fact is, that using tools and 'toys' in your psychic development makes it fun. When something is fun to learn, it is easier to learn. The tools in these pages are not crutches – they are devices that will help you to expand your abilities into new areas of expertise. Some of these tools will merely be one more step in your learning process while others will become lifelong friends that you rely on to help you to get more accurate psychic information for yourself, friends, and clients.

Here's another good thing about working with psychic tools – many people that you read will relate better to your information if they see you working with a tool of some sort while you read them. Some people simply find you more believable if they see a tool in your hands than if you are simply talking to them. Additionally, you may read some people who are difficult to connect with. Perhaps their emotionalism is in the way, or they are fearful of getting a reading, so they are shut down and are shutting you out psychically at the same time. When you work with tools it is easy to get past these blocks. It is as if the people you are reading focus on the tool you are using, and drops the wall they have put up to you! So, even readers who don't normally work with psychic tools need to know how and to have a favorite that they can employ in an emergency!

Many professional readers work with psychometry and the pendulum as a routine procedure. Most psychics are accomplished astral travelers who not only use their astral travel in their daily lives to enhance their life experience, they also continue their learning in classes on the astral. You will be amazed that as you learn these techniques you will begin to have similar experiences yourself!

Everything you will learn in the following pages will be fun. Some of it will challenge you. All of it will stimulate your psychic development in both conscious and unconscious ways. The more you practice with these tools and the more you do the exercises in these pages, the more beneficial the information will be for you.

These tools are not just aids to your readings; they are tools for self-development. Use them frequently, use them wisely, and use them well.

Chapter 1

The Art of Psychometry

If you have studied Psychic Development Level 2, you already did a version of psychometry when you learned to feel and read the auras around people. In this chapter you will be learning a more traditional approach to psychometry.

Psychometry is most commonly associated with tuning in and reading the vibration attached to an object. Learning to psychometrize an object is actually a great deal easier than learning to psychometrize and read the aura or vibration of a person. Objects do not change or block their vibration, as people sometimes do.

Even if you did not study the aura reading techniques in Psychic Development Level 2, you will still find that psychometrizing an object comes to you very easily... psychometry is a natural human ability, and I have yet to find someone who cannot do it at all, though students do have varying levels of proficiency.

Of course studying the meditative tools in Psychic Development Levels 1 and 2 is an aid to creating your ability for strong focus, and learning to feel the difference between your own vibration and that of another person or an object. So, I still do highly recommend you go back and begin your studies there, if you haven't already done so.

Let's talk for a moment about the vibration around objects. Everything has an aura or energy field surrounding it; people, animals, houses, objects, etc. The greater the electromagnetic charge an object is holding, the stronger its vibration, or its aura, will be and the easier it will be to feel. When you do psychometry, you are tuning into this aura or vibrational energy field and you are interpreting the feelings you get from the field into words that describe the object's past, or its owner, or something else about it. You can also use your link to the object to focus into the future life of the person who owns the object. The psychic gift being employed here is empathy, the psychic ability being used is clairsentience, and the tool is psychometry.

Empathy, Clairsentience and Psychometry

Empathy is a psychic gift linked to the emotions. Everyone is empathic to some degree, but many people are born with this gift already well developed. These people, who are called *empaths* are sensitive to other people's emotions to a fault. If you cry, they cry. If you are happy, they are happy. If you are mad, they are mad. I discussed the gift of empathy at great length in Psychic Development Level 1, and explained that untrained empaths are both a danger to themselves and to other people because their emotions are essentially beyond their own control.

However, a trained empath has the ability to become an excellent psychometrist and aura reader as the electromagnetic substance of the aura and the vibrations around objects are very similar to the vibration created by strong emotion. In fact, you will find that objects that have been owned by a person with powerful emotions are always easier to psychometrize than objects that are new, or have just lain in a drawer for a long time.

So, if you already know that if you have a fair to strong gift of empathy, you should expect that you will do quite well with psychometry.

Clairsentience, or clear feeling, is the psychic ability you will be employing to do your psychometry. It gives you your ability to actually hold an object and tune in to the vibration it is emitting. I will be presenting several exercises in this chapter that will help you to do this quite easily. Once you learn to use your clairsentience, performing psychometry is actually very easy. This is why readers who have already mastered the techniques presented in Level 2 will very quickly do well at this.

But before you actually learn the process, let's take a moment more to examine the principle of vibration, what kinds of vibrations you may find around objects, what vibrations are easy to read, and which types of objects you should decline to read. The field of psychometry is very broad. An entire book could be written on it... but this discussion will at least give you a good foundation to work with.

The Principle of Vibration

You can think of the vibration an object emits as being a record of its history, or its memory. All objects, regardless of how insignificant, have this. This principle is very similar to the concept that the cells of your body retain a memory of everything you have ever experienced. People who have had rolfing done (deep tissue massage) will be familiar with the experience of having all kinds of emotions from the past that you had totally forgotten surface during a rolfing session, as the deep massage literally squeezed the memory out of the cells. It is essentially the same with the cellular memory of the object. An object remembers everything it has ever experienced at the cellular level, and its electromagnetic vibration is the vibratory language that tells the world of that experience. All the psychic needs to do is to tune into it and read it, to find out whatever he or she needs to know about the object's experience.

I remember when I was first learning this skill I asked a friend to give me an object to psychometrize. She had trouble coming up with something that wasn't her own. I asked her to give me an object that wasn't hers... if I knew it was hers I wouldn't have known if the information I got was accurate because I knew her too well. She finally located something in the bottom of her purse. I had her place it in an envelope so that I couldn't see what it was (I didn't want its physical appearance to distract me from the actual energy reading I wanted to do). Well, I struggled and struggled to get ANY impression. I used all the techniques I had learned. And then I did them again. Finally I said, "I'm sorry, the only thing I can get from this is a shopping cart, like in a grocery store." She burst out laughing. When I looked in the envelope, I found a small box of birthday candles. She told me she had just bought them at the supermarket for her son's upcoming birthday. Not more than a half an hour earlier they had been in the bottom of a shopping cart, exactly where I saw them.

As you see, the history of the box of candles was somewhat limited. I saw them in the shopping cart because that was the only real point of emotional tension that they had been subjected to... the only place some additional energy had been added into them. I suppose if I was really good at the time I might have seen the assembly line where they were made. But it was a person connected to them that I was looking for, and my friend had been the only person to really come in contact with them. And she had just put them in a shopping cart. Hence, my simple but accurate reading of the box of candles.

You can see from this example that simple generic objects have a much less intense vibration than objects that have been owned by someone, and that objects that have been prized possessions, or that have been worn by someone, will have a stronger vibration than ones that have merely been used as decorations.

Most of the time people who ask you to do psychometry don't want to know anything about the object itself (although there are occasional exceptions to this)... they usually want to know something about the person who owned the object. Because of this, it is important that they choose something with a strong connection to the person they want to know about. And the strongest of all connections is an emotional link.

Jewelry items such as wedding rings and watches are excellent subjects for psychometry. Clothing can also be a good medium to use, but it will not maintain as strong a connection if it has been laundered. Any personal items that the person your client wants to know about carried on his or her body is a good link to that person that you can psychometrize. Stay away from psychometrizing things like money though. Money has been handled by so many people throughout its history that it is very hard to pick one person out of the many who have carried it. It is also treated very impersonally. The only time money is a good focus for psychometry is if it is a person's lucky coin you are working with! Needless to say, things like hair, fingernails, or teeth are very good to use as a focus, too. They literally contain the DNA of the person, so they are really the very best link of all! Photographs are also good, but make sure the subject is in the photo by himself or herself or you could confuse the vibration with someone else in it.

Objects with a long history will also seem to project at you the strongest people that have owned them, or the most emotional. For example, when psychometrizing the ring of a young man I knew, I came up with an older gentleman, who had built his own business and had a very strong character. I described him quite accurately, and said to the young man, "I didn't know your father left you that ring." He replied, that yes, his dad did leave him the ring, but my description was not of his dad... it was his great grandfather, who had been the third owner of the ring. The reason why the great grandfather was the one most strongly associated with the ring at the time could have been his strength of character, or the fact that the young man was a lot like him, thereby bringing that character out of the ring, or that something in me resonated to that particular owner of the ring.

All of these factors conspire to affect your psychometry. This is why several different psychics can do psychometry on the same object and come up with different information. It will not necessarily be in conflict though at the time it may seem so... it is just different.

It is also possible to psychometrize the electromagnetic vibration in a room, although this is more commonly referred to as using your clairsentience because it is usually done through direct sensing, as opposed to touching or holding anything. Many people have this ability naturally quite strongly developed, and are very environmentally sensitive as a result. I recall entering a large drawing room in an old mansion in Williamsburg, Virginia, many years ago, for example, and seeing and feeling as if the room was filled with people dancing. I later found out that in the 1700's the room was used for just such social purposes. It was not ghosts I was seeing and feeling, but rather the remnants of the vibration that so many people, dancing with high emotions so often, had left behind. Similarly, many people use this same ability to sense the feeling in an environment as they walk into it, quickly determining if it is a healthy one for them or not. Such people, in whom clairsentience is well developed, usually know immediately upon meeting someone if that person is good for them or not as well. Everyone can develop these abilities; that is what this book is all about. But there are some who already have them well developed, and will be more interested in learning to control them than in how to do them.

You can also psychometrize a chair just by sitting in it and relaxing into its vibration. This is why you like one chair better than another, though they may look exactly alike!

You will also note, if you look around the room you are in right now, and allow yourself to sense the various objects in the room, that certain objects really do seem to have a much stronger feeling of being present in the room than others. This is one way of determining which objects in your environment, or even which rooms in your home, retain the strongest electromagnetic vibration. Generally speaking, these will be objects that are family heirlooms, or that you have attached emotional significance to, or the particular pieces of furniture that you use the most, or the rooms that you spend the most time in. I am always amazed for example, that in most people's homes the strongest waves of energy are usually collected around the TV! That is because most people sit in front of it looking at it for hours on end, sending their wandering thoughts to it as their minds skim through all the emotional issues of the day. The thought-energy literally collects around the TV, and the chair you are sitting in while you project it.

Are you a collector of antiques? Or are you a thrift-shop junkie? If you are, chances are you are collecting objects that are steeped in the vibrations of people you don't even know or have never even met.

Now that you are aware that all objects and all environments retain both vibration and a memory of everything they have experienced, you should be asking yourself some important questions, such as, "How will the vibration of an object affect me?" and "Can I clear the vibration, the memory, from an object or a room?"

How the Vibration of an Object or a Place Can Affect You

The vibrations of objects can definitely affect you. In essence, there is actually some substance behind the old *Curse of the Mummy* movies. Although it is possible to clear collected excess vibration from an object or a place, it is not possible to erase the memory of what it has experienced. Much like a person can be induced to forget unpleasant experiences through hypnosis or trauma, an object can be charged to cover or conceal its memory of a person or an event. But the actual memory, in either case, cannot be removed and will still have an unconscious affect. In most cases, such blocking of memories is simply impractical, if not totally undesirable. Yet the vibrations on the objects you possess can definitely have a strong affect on you.

If you have a family heirloom that makes you feel uncomfortable, I suggest you give it away. If you pick up an item in a resale shop that you think is pretty, but each time you wear it or use it you find you get a headache, give it away. If an item a friend has given you makes you feel too close to him (or her) or too much like him when you wear it, give it back, or give it away. In each of these cases, the vibration on the object, and its memory are influencing your thoughts and feelings in a way that is not good for you. On the other hand, if you always feel happy when you carry a certain object, or stronger, or more confident, consider the vibration of that object good for you!

You should be particularly careful of buying or otherwise acquiring used divinatory items like rune stones or Tarot cards, or any items that have been used in magic ritual. You'd be better off actually, to just pass them up. This includes pieces of the Great Pyramid, folks, if they are real. Any object that has been used as a focus for psychic work has become VERY highly charged with the original owner's energy, and if you use the tool yourself, before long you may actually begin to think and act like that person. The object, in this case Tarot cards, for example, will quite literally download the original owner's personality on you. Objects that have been the source of that kind of intense focus literally become a repository for the former owner's energy. In the case of bringing a piece of a pyramid or temple home with you, realize that you have no way of knowing if the object was charged magically or not because usually such use of energy is undetectable except by its results. You would really only know if you had a magically charged item if you began to have some weird urges that were totally outside the range of your normal behavior.

Objects passed on to you from people who have died tragically or who had very bad personality disorders can also have a very detrimental affect on you and your environment. Let me recount a rather frightening example from the life of one of my students.

She came to me to discuss a problem with her son. It seems her sister's son was murdered in a knife fight. He was not a good person; he hung out with the wrong people, couldn't hold a job, was involved with drugs and gangland activities, had quit school, had an attitude problem, mistreated his family and friends, and had been in and out of prison. At the time he was killed he was wearing a black leather bomber jacket. His mother, knowing her sister's son liked the jacket, gave it to him rather than throwing it out. That is when the young boys problems began. He wore the jacket all the time. He began to develop an attitude problem; played hooky from school; his grade-point average dropped; he began to hang out with a rough crowd, etc. In short, he began to act just as his wayward cousin had. My student knew something was going on and suspected it might be connected to the jacket. My suggestion was to take the jacket away. When she finally was able to peel it off of him (literally) she ended up burning it just so that he couldn't get it back, he had become that attached to it. Sure enough, after the jacket was removed from her son's life he went back to being the normal and nice kid he had been. A very harsh example, and a very close call for the young man.

Now you might be asking at this point, why not just wash the jacket? Or clear it? Or put a block on it? The answer is that you can't erase the memory of who that dead boy was. Washing clears excess energy, but doesn't erase memory. The same thing is true with clearing. I will show you some clearing techniques later on that are wonderful for grounding the excess energy in an environment, or on an object, but these techniques do not erase memory. Even with a complete block some of that behavior was bound to leak through. Or, if you totally blocked the vibration on the jacket, it would lose all personality and become undesirable anyway. To learn how to apply a charge or block (essentially the same thing) I suggest you study some of Scott Cunningham's books... that information is beyond the scope of this book.

By now you have an understanding of what empathy, clairsentience, and psychometry are, and you understand how objects and environments accumulate memory as vibration. Your next step is to learn how to read that vibration and turn it into words that the person whose object you are reading can understand. You are ready to learn the process of psychometry.

As a beginner learning psychometry you are best off having your partner place the object he wants you to read in an envelope, so that you will not be distracted by what the object is. For example, if I ask you to psychometrize a key for me, it is likely that I know what the key opens, and I certainly know it is a key. I most likely want you to use the key as a link to tune in to the person who normally carries the key, and to tell me something about him or her. Eventually, you will not even register what the object is when you do psychometry; it will merely be a link. But for now, use an envelope. Also, the object should belong to someone your partner can give feedback about.

How to Do Psychometry

In order to psychometrize an object, you must first merge your vibration with the objects in order to be able to feel and read it. The diagram below, a variation repeated from Psychic Development Level 2, shows graphically what is happening as you do this. Following the diagram is a guided meditation that will help you to do this automatically.

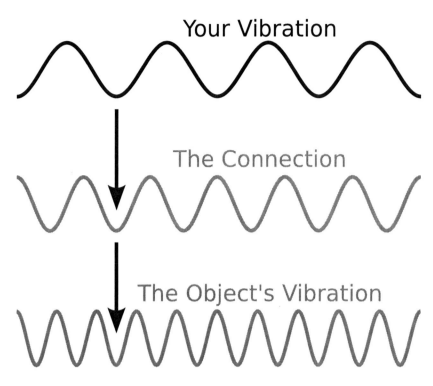

Your Vibration

The Connection

The Object's Vibration

Figure 1: Merging Your Vibration With That of an Object

Exercise #1: Guided Meditation to Merge Your Energy With That of an Object

---

1. As you did in Psychic Development Level 2, you first need to put on your protective bracelets or gloves. These are protections that you visualize actually being on your hands and that allow you to read the object while keeping its energy out of your own body. NEVER do psychometry without first doing this!

2. Take three deep diaphragmatic breaths as you ground and center. Release all of the worries of the day. You may choose to use your worry box from Psychic Development Level 1 to put your concerns into, and lock them away to clear your mind.

3. Now, focus your attention on the envelope holding the object you will psychometrize. Put one hand on each side of the envelope, and gently rub it between your palms.

4. First, concentrate on the physical characteristics of the object through the envelope. Note if it is heavy, or light; big, or small; rough, or smooth.

5. Now, take another deep breath and let your consciousness drop down into stillness as you exhale. Let go of all thought. Feel the characteristics of the

energy of the object. Weigh it again – does it feel heavier or lighter than before? Does it feel bigger or smaller than it did the first time? Does it have a color? Let your mind drop deeper into the color with each breath you take. Relax into it for a few minutes, until you feel that you are making a strong connection to the energy of the object.

6. Notice the physical sensations in your own body that you experience while you are holding the objects. This is very important. It is your reality check. Does your link to the object make your breath heavier or lighter? Does your heart beat faster or slower? Are you perspiring more heavily? At this point, if you do not like the way the object is making you feel, or if you have negative or depressing feelings about it, lay it aside. Do not ever try to read an object that you do not feel you should read!

7. If you still feel good about the object at this point, you can begin your reading. The steps to take to do your reading of the object are outlined in the next exercise.

There are two important points I want to emphasize relative to the above exercise. Both of these points have to do with protection during psychometry. Your protection is only as good as your ability to follow the rules. Please do not ever do psychometry without your protective gloves. And NEVER forget to do your reality check or listen to its results! I'll show you why in two short examples, both taken from my own experience.

First, there was the time I was trying to read an object that seemed to have no vibration. (Remember, I told you above that magically charged objects often appear to have no vibration. Well, I didn't know that back then.) A gentleman who was interested in dating me at the time had asked me to psychometrize it and it was important to me to impress him. I knew I was good at this. (Rule #1 – NEVER let your ego dictate your behavior! It ALWAYS gets you into trouble!) I actually had put my gloves on. But when I couldn't read the object I went deeper, and tried harder, and went deeper, and eventually completely opened up to absorb the energy of the object, even to taking off those gloves. I never did get anything from the item. I finally gave it back to him, but about five minutes later, the charge that had been on the item struck. All of a sudden, all I could think about was this guy, in all kinds of compromising situations. I knew immediately what had happened, that he had charged the object to create an obsession in me for him. And, of course, that meant that I would have died at that point before I'd ever date him, so his magic didn't work. But It took me about three days of salt baths, sleeping with my hand on the floor, and salt sprinkled under the sheets I slept on before I was finally able to clear him from my mind. So, DON'T take those gloves off... and DON'T be a sucker either!

The second incident I want to relate to you is actually far more likely to occur to you. It involved not paying attention to my reality check. A student brought me an ID bracelet to psychometrize. Since she was a student, I didn't question whether she would bring me something that would have a really bad vibration – I assumed she would know better. So when my reality check said, "This is really bad, you don't want to tune into this," I ignored it, and went on to drop even deeper into alpha state to do the reading. And instantly felt a knifelike pain enter my heart, and was enveloped by negative and evil feelings of rage and anger at the same time. I quickly put the bracelet down and grounded my hands on the floor, breathing white light in through my Crown Center, spreading it through my body and pushing it down and out through my palms and feet on the floor. Then I asked her why she had given me a piece of jewelry someone was killed in to read. This was the woman I mentioned earlier in the chapter, whose son had inherited the leather jacket from his wayward cousin. It was my student's way of testing to see if the jacket could have the negative feelings attached to it that she suspected it did. Her test was an accurate way to arrive at this information, but extremely rude and insensitive. She only realized that after the fact. So even if you know a person well, don't be gullible. Make sure the object you are reading is safe to read – do your reality check and listen if it tells you, "No, don't read this!"

Let me tell you, after that experience I have nothing except deep admiration for the many psychics who work selflessly undercover with law-enforcement agencies to handle these types of items on a fairly regular basis. It takes a very special type of empath to be able to merge with those negative vibrations and not become contaminated. And psychics who work with the police MUST be selfless, because for their own protection, they must stay very much behind the scenes. It is truly a job of service, with little or no recognition attached to it, and a lot of wading through other people's pain to get to the truth. Unless you are that special type of psychic, and feel a strong calling toward it, I advise you to steer clear of that type of work.

Reading the Object

Let's move on to doing the reading once you've tuned into the object. As I explained in Psychic Development Level 2, when you first tune in to a person or an object, you will receive an immediate flood of information that you will have to sort through and present to the person you are reading in some kind of understandable order. But once you make your way through that initial flood of information, which you may receive as feelings, pictures, words, or emotions, you will find yourself just waiting with no other input coming in. It is as if the object has released the immediate set of memories or other information that you were capable of making a connection to, and nothing more will be forthcoming unless you supply the next key to open up more of its information files. If you are lucky, you are reading for an extremely open person, who is not afraid to ask you some questions, which will help you to access those areas within the object where the answers to those questions lie. But in most cases, your partner or client is not going to be such a help to you. Usually he is going to simply look at you with an expectant tell-me-what-you-get look on his face. So, it will have to be you who ask yourself the necessary questions to bring out that information your client wants to know about.

Doing psychometry is a lot like surfing the Internet. When you initially log onto a site you immediately are swamped with information about the site... but unless you continue to surf, you can't get any further information. The questions you need to ask yourself to surf through the electromagnetic energy memory of the object are actually very similar to the kinds of questions you would ask yourself when you are surfing the Web looking for something. You need to keep the focus of what you are looking for uppermost in your mind, and ask yourself questions that gradually bring you closer to an answer.

It does help if before you do a psychometry reading you ask the person getting the reading if he wants to know about a specific person connected to the item, or if he wants to know about the item itself. That at least helps you to focus initially in the right direction. And since there can be many people connected to certain objects, you should also ask your client, after you receive that initial burst of information, whether it makes sense to him, and if you are getting the person he wants to know about. If you are not, you can always let go of the person you got and look to see if someone else comes through strongly. If you don't get anyone else, you may have to ask the client whom it is he is trying to get information about, through the object, and then see if you can't use the object as a link to the person. If you still can't, you need to return the item to the person and tell him it just is not working for you as a focus. It may be that the person he wants you to connect with through the object did not have a strong link to the object, or subconsciously does not want to be read and is blocking you. This leads me to another important point: the subject of ethics.

Ethics in Psychometry

Ask yourself if you would go uninvited into a person's house, and go through all of his (or her) most personal items just to see what you could find out about him. Now ask yourself if you would appreciate someone invading your own privacy that way. Doing a psychic reading, uninvited, is essentially the same thing.

You will occasionally use psychometry to strengthen your link to the person you are reading – for example, a person whose reading you are doing may give you his own ring to hold during the session to make it easier for you to link into him. Or if you are doing a reading by mail or phone, your client may send you a photograph of him to use as a focus. In either of these cases, there is no ethical problem. The person getting the reading inviting you into his own life for a look around is between you and him.

But most of the time when you do psychometry it is going to be on a third party's belonging. Usually, your client is bringing you something that belongs to a friend or relative he wants to know something about. Here is where the problem of ethics comes up. Some psychics absolutely refuse to do psychometry on a third party's belonging, and resolve the ethical problem that way. Others will only do it on an object belonging to someone who has passed on, or in an emergency situation (i.e., if someone has disappeared). My own resolution is that I will give information about the third party to my client, but only information that the third party has either asked to know about, or that has a direct affect on my client. For example, I might tell a girl a boy she is dating is dating around, but I would not give her information on the other girls he is dating. Do you see the difference? Giving her the information that yes, he is dating other girls helps her to handle the relationship intelligently and protect herself emotionally. Giving her the information about the other girls only fuels her jealousy and creates a focus of bad feeling in her relationship with the young man. In fact, doing that could interfere in the relationship in a way that would lead to its early ending.

You will really have to sort this out yourself. But do keep in mind that a psychic reader has a responsibility to deliver information responsibly. When you do a reading you should always ask yourself if you feel that the information the client is looking for is really right for you to give – provided you can access it anyway! If giving the information the client wants makes you feel uncomfortable, that is a good sign you should not be doing it. If you can ask yourself the question, would it bother me if someone was asking these questions about me, and come up with a 'no' answer, go ahead and read the object. But if your answer is yes, you should give it back to the client and decline to do the reading.

Unfortunately, you are going to be surprised how many of your friends and family members want you to use this tool to spy on people, once they discover how accurate it can be!

Well, enough of ethics. I'm sure you can figure the rest out for yourself. Let's move on to actually doing the reading. Exercise #2 (below) builds on Exercise #1 to get you into doing an actual reading. Remember, this is only a guideline and when you do an actual reading you will have to supply your own self-guiding questions pertinent to the object and the information the client is looking for.

Exercise #2: Guided Visualization to Lead You Through a Psychometry Reading

(Steps 1 through 7 are identical to Exercise #1)

1. Put on your protective bracelets or gloves. NEVER do psychometry without first doing this!

2. Take three deep diaphragmatic breaths as you ground and center. Release all of the worries of the day. Use your worry to put your concerns into, and lock them away to clear your mind.

3. Now, focus your attention on the envelope holding the object you will psychometrize. As you gain more experience you may psychometrize the object directly, but for now continue to use an envelope. Put one hand on each side of the envelope, and gently rub it between your palms.

4. First, concentrate on the physical characteristics of the object through the envelope. Note if it is heavy, or light; big, or small; rough, or smooth.

5. Now, take another deep breath and let your consciousness drop down into stillness as you exhale. Let go of all thought. Feel the characteristics of the energy of the object. Weigh it again – does it feel heavier or lighter than before? Does it feel bigger or smaller than it did the first time? Does it have a color? Let your mind drop deeper into the color with each breath you take. Relax into it for a few minutes, until you feel that you are making a strong connection to the energy of the object.

6. Notice the physical sensations in your own body that you experience while you are holding the objects. This is very important. It is your reality check. Does your link to the object make your breath heavier or lighter? Does your heart beat faster or slower? Are you perspiring more heavily? At this point, if you do not like the way the object is making you feel, or if you have negative or depressing feelings about it, lay it aside.

   If you still feel good about the object at this point, you can begin your reading.

7. Go back to perceiving the color you associated with the object. Use it as a focus. Continue with deep diaphragmatic breaths. As you do, allow your mind to travel deeper into the color. As you drift to the bottom of the color, you will see a person associated with the object.

8. Immediately describe what you see and feel about the person you have focused on. If you are not clear initially, you can achieve a stronger connection and greater clarity by asking yourself questions: Is the person you see male or female, adult or child, big or small? Can you see more about his or her physical appearance – what color is the hair, what kind of clothing is he or she wearing?

9. Extend your mental questions to include where this person is. What do you see around the person? Is he or she indoors or outdoors? At work or at home? What do you see him or her doing?

10. Now expand your questions into more emotionally based areas. Can you feel what is important to the person right now? Can you tell if he or she is happy or sad, or calm or tense? If so, what about? Do you get a sense of any pain or discomfort from the person, or any sense of illness around him or her? If so, what does it concern?

11. See if you can get information on this person's relationships. Do you see any people around this person that he or she may be close to? Can you describe any of these people physically? What do you feel is the nature of the relationship? Is it good or bad for the person?

12. Now see if you can take a mental walk into the future of the person associated with this object. Look with your mind five years into the future. What do you see this person doing in five years? Is he or she still living in the same place? Working the same job? In the same relationships?

13. Finally, take a deep breath and release the energy. Put the object down. Your hands will feel hot, so shake them out, and then place them on the floor to ground. Visualize white light coming down through your Crown Center, filling your body, and flowing out through your arms and hands into the ground, carrying any excess energy you may have picked up from the object with it. Take a deep breath and blow the remnants of any excess energy into the ground through your hands.

14. Get some feedback from your partner/client. Feedback is important because it lets you know what you need to work on, as well as gives you positive reinforcement when you are correct. Ask your partner to confirm any areas he or she is unsure about, and get back to you on it later.

Psychometry and Trance

Psychometry is one of the tools that some people will find leads them into a state of trance. What I mean by this is that some people who are natural *trance mediums* will tend to drop so deeply into a rapport with the object that they lose self-awareness entirely, and will have no recollection of anything they have said to their partner/client when they are done with the reading. Some of these people may even be able to use the object as a direct link to its owner that is so strong that they will begin to take on the owner's characteristics, perhaps even speaking in their voice as they do the reading, or even speaking in another language. Some of these owners may be alive, while some may be dead. Many people are attracted to becoming trance mediums because to them it is easy. All they need to do is to step aside, and let someone else come in and do the reading for them. They get the accolades without having to do the work.

I want to strongly warn you AGAINST doing this. If you feel yourself going too deep and losing your self-awareness you need to bring yourself back up by changing your focus to the superficial characteristics of the object. Open your eyes for a moment and look at your partner/client. That will help get you grounded in YOU again. Here are the reasons I am so against this.

Firstly, just putting on the glove-protection described earlier in this chapter will not protect against this if you go too deep, nor will it protect you from becoming inhabited by someone else whom you will certainly not want staying to take up residence. Remember, *anyone's* energy in you does not feel right because it is not you. And a foreign energy inside your body over a period of time will burn out your nerve circuits the same way running 100 volts through a 20-volt line would burn out the wiring. And until you learn much more serious protection, you would not be able to keep an evil person, or someone who would merely use the connection to drain your energy, out.

Secondly, let me tell you right away that I am NOT an advocate of trance mediumship in ANY form. And that is for one glaringly important reason – it kills the medium. Every single trance medium that I have known or read about has died at an early age. The most famous of these, Edgar Cayce, died in his early 40's. His guides warned him that if he continued to do this work, it would kill him. Yet he did continue, probably believing that his work was more important than his life. Another famous trance medium was Jane Roberts, author of the Seth books. She died at age 39. The list of people who have done this kind of work and either died young or began to fake it is staggering. Therefore I recommend to my students that they avoid it. If your goal is to be a psychic medium, you can achieve that goal safely without becoming a trance medium, by continuing on with your studies in the Anastasi System.

Clearing an Object

I mentioned earlier in this chapter that although it is impossible to clear away an object's memory, it is possible to clear and ground it of excess energy, or particularly negative vibration. I will give you a brief list of grounding and clearing techniques you can use here:

1. If the object is durable and waterproof, place it under running water for about 10 minutes. The flow of the water creates a stream of negatively charged ions that pulls the excess charge from the object and clears it.

2. You can do the same thing as in #1 using the water from a running stream if you live near one. This is particularly effective, since resting the object on the dirt or rock bottom of the stream also grounds it. Remember to secure it in place if you do this.

3. Soak the object in a cup of water with three pinches of sea salt, rock or Kosher salt stirred three times, overnight. If the object is too large to soak, you can sprinkle the salt and water over it.

4. Lay the object on a bed of sea salt, rock or Kosher salt overnight.

5. Bury the object beneath a pine tree (be sure to put it into a plastic bag first) overnight.

6. Clear the object with sage, camphor, pine, or frankincense and myrrh incense by smudging it with the incense – i.e., making sure the incense drifts all around it, usually in a clockwise direction.

*These are only some of the more common clearing and grounding techniques. They by no means exhaust the large array of methods being used.

These techniques of clearing will make an object feel better, and return it to its normal state if it has acquired a dirty feel to it. As a matter of fact, doing this with your own personal items of jewelry, crystals, etc., will keep them feeling new and special to you. But they will not erase from the object any of the people or situations it has experienced. As I stated earlier, it is not possible to do that. An object's memory can be blocked or concealed by magically overlaying it using a ritual to charge it (consult Scott Cunningham, Lori Cabot, Maria Gonzalez-Whippler or other reputable authors of magic books for the proper techniques to use) or by doing energy work on it to pull its vibration into a different pattern. The latter is a technique I described in Psychic Development Level 2 when I discussed techniques of empathic healing. The same technique used for healing can be used for altering the vibration of an object. I urge you to NOT do this though on an object you think was magically charged or that contains great negativity because the risk of your absorbing the negativity is far too great. It is safer to use a magical technique if you feel you must do this.

Clearing a Space

Knowing how to clear a space can be very important, especially if you are ever asked to do psychic work outside your home or in an unprotected environment – this is not unusual at all for professional psychics as a matter of fact. Here are some quick and easy ways to clear a space around the table or place at which you will be working:

1. Prepare some salt and water, as above, and sprinkle it on the floor clockwise around the place you will be working, starting from the East, if you know it.

2. Sprinkle some salt clockwise around your workplace, starting from the East.

3. Ring a small bell in the four directions, starting with East.

4. Use a feather fan to fan negativity from the area around your workspace, starting in the East and moving clockwise.

5. Use smoke from incense or a smudge stick to push negativity out, carrying it clockwise around your workplace.

6. Place a cleared crystal in each of the four quarters, standing for each direction, to block out negativity.

*Of course these are only a few of the many ways of quickly clearing your space. In Psychic Development Level 4 you will learn still another method that involves energy work alone.

Choosing a Direction to Face when Doing Your Psychic Work

People are direction-sensitive. Many people do not realize this. But it is a good thing to recognize and to work with this because if you know which direction works best for you, you will be able to improve your overall performance in everything you do.

Similar to a pigeon, we actually have large amounts of iron in our sinus area that makes us sensitive to True North. Although most of us have not had the opportunity to experiment with this, many studies have been conducted that determined that people have essentially the same sort of homing instinct that messenger birds have.

It is this homing instinct and directional sensitivity that actually allows you to do a better reading if you are facing a direction that is comfortable and natural for you, and even to get a better night's sleep, if the crown of your head is pointing to either the North or the East. Carlos Castanada pointed out in his earliest books that the energy field of the earth has places that are good for you, and places that are bad for you. If a place feels bad, try to clear it, using the above techniques. If that doesn't work, leave it. Trust your instincts. And learn which direction you resonate best to. Be sure to be facing that direction any time you do your psychic work, and you will get better results. You can also face that same direction when meditating, and you will be surprised to see that you get a deeper meditation as well.

Here is a simple exercise to find the best direction to face when doing your psychic work.

Exercise #3: Finding Your Best Direction

1. Stand in the center of your room. Close your eyes, and reach your arms out in front of you, hands extended.

2. Sensitize your fingertips to the air around you. Put your attention into your fingertips until you can actually feel the currents of air, no matter how slight, moving across them. Feel them begin to tingle.

3. Now turn slowly in place moving gradually in a 360-degree circle, still holding your hands outstretched. Feel the changing currents in the space around you as you do this.

4. Eventually, as you keep turning you will feel a pull in a certain direction. Open your eyes and note where you are facing. Check the direction against a directional compass. This is the direction you should be facing whenever you do your psychic or meditation work.

End of Chapter Exercises

1. As in Psychic Development Levels 1 and 2, continue to record and interpret your dreams. They will give you good insight into your daily life, may contain precognitive information, as well as possible messages from your Higher Self.

2. Record all of your psychic experiences. This positive reinforcement helps your development.

3. Continue your telepathy exercises from Psychic Development Levels 1 and 2 with a partner. For this current exercise send and receive a scene to which you will attach a feeling – such as rocking in a sailboat. Don't forget to remote view your partner.

4. Do psychometry on as many objects as you can to practice. Be sure to arrange to get feedback.

5. Complete the Psychic Development Aptitude Exercise on the next page. If you like, purchase or make up your own flashcards to go with it. Flashcards that go with this exercise are also available for instant download on my Web site, free of charge, at www.SandyAnastasi.com. This will show improvements if you did the exercise in Psychic Development Level 1, and if not, will form a baseline for you to compare your improvement against when we repeat the exercise in Chapter 6. I've included instructions, so if you are a newcomer to this, you'll be able to follow right along.

If you did the *End of Chapter Exercises* in the last chapter of Psychic Development Level 2, you remote viewed three envelopes that had been placed in three different locations with three different items in them. If you didn't do it then, do it now. Then read the answer below. If you did this on your own, working with a friend who hid envelopes for you, you will have different answers. If you did our exercise, you will have remote-viewed backward in time and these are your answers:

1. Envelope 1 is a pink 9"x6" envelope containing a paper bookmark from Starchild Books. It is leaning against the side of a window frame, standing upright on the sill.

2. Envelope 2 is a green 5"x6" envelope containing a pink eraser. It is inside of a drawer containing silverware, on the right side. The drawer is underneath a coffee pot.

3. Envelope 3 is another 5"x6" envelope, gray in color. It is lying on a white bookcase, second shelf from the top, and contains a bobby pin.

The Psychic Development Aptitude Exercise

Your Psychic Development Aptitude Exercise looks more difficult to score than it is. Some simple instructions follow.

You should either be sitting opposite your partner, or have him on the phone or use a chat room Internet connection. You will both do the exercise; first one sends, the other receives, and then you reverse roles. You should each have a score sheet. On your score sheet you'll notice a space for the name of the sender and the receiver. That's because you're BOTH being tested. The receiver can't receive if the sender didn't send correctly! When you're done with the exercise, you should make photocopies of both forms so you can each have a record of your performance sending, as well as receiving. You should photocopy the form in this book and keep one in reserve for future copying.

Divide your deck of cards into two sections, black and white, and colors. If you didn't get the cards, you'll be working directly from the form, which is already divided into these two sections – black and white on the left side, colors on the right.

Start with cards numbered 1-25, the black and white ones. The shapes on them will be a square, circle, star, or triangle. The sender should shuffle the cards to take them out of order. Each has a number in the lower right corner that mirrors the same shape and number on the score sheet. If you are working straight from the score sheet, just focus on the shapes randomly.

Your partner should say the first shape that he or she thinks of.

To record his choice, look down the score sheet to the number of the card you projected; if the shape is correct, put a check in the column next to it. If it was incorrect, draw in the proper shape. Sometimes your partner calls out a wrong shape, and then you turn over the next card only to see that shape was next. That's precognition. Put a check next to the shape in the precognitive column.

Likewise, your partner may call out the correct shape only after you've already put the card you were working with down, and drawn the next one! That's post-cognitive. Note it with a check next to the card in the post-cognitive column.

When you've done the black and white shapes, you're ready to move onto the colored shapes, numbers 26 through 50. The scoring is the same, but it's a bit more time consuming because you have to score the correct/incorrect, precognitive and post-cognitive for the colors as well. The colors this exercise uses are red, blue, yellow, green, orange, and purple.

The exercise is on the next page.

Psychic Development Exercise

Date: _____ Sender Name: _____ Receiver Name: _____

Card Number	Shape	Check if Correct / Note Shape If Incorrect	Check If Precognitive	Check If Post-cognitive
1	○			
2	△			
3	□			
4	○			
5	☆			
6	☆			
7	○			
8	□			
9	△			
10	○			
11	☆			
12	□			
13	△			
14	○			
15	☆			
16	△			
17	○			
18	□			
19	□			
20	○			
21	☆			
22	△			
23	○			
24	△			
25	○			

Card Number	Shape	Check if Correct / Note Shape If Incorrect	Check If Precognitive	Check If Post-cognitive	Color	Check if Correct / Note Color If Incorrect	Check If Precognitive	Check If Post-cognitive	Note If Both Are Correct Now, Pre and Post
26	□				Blue				
27	○				Orange				
28	△				Blue				
29	☆				Purple				
30	□				Yellow				
31	○				Green				
32	☆				Orange				
33	△				Red				
34	○				Red				
35	△				Purple				
36	□				Green				
37	□				Yellow				
38	☆				Red				
39	○				Orange				
40	△				Blue				
41	○				Red				
42	☆				Yellow				
43	□				Purple				
44	△				Yellow				
45	□				Red				
46	☆				Green				
47	○				Blue				
48	△				Purple				
49	△				Green				
50	☆				Red				

Score Sheet For Black And White Only

List Patterns Below

Score: _____

Number Correct: _____

Number Pre: _____

Number Post: _____

Score Sheet For Color Only

List Patterns: _____

Number of Shapes Correct: _____

Number of Colors Correct: _____

Number of Shapes Precognitive: _____

Number of Colors Precognitive: _____

Number of Shapes Postcognitive: _____

Number of Colors Postcognitive: _____

Number of Both Color And Shape:

Now: _____

Pre: _____

Post: _____

Grand Total: _____

Table 1: The Psychic Development Aptitude Exercise
A free, printable copy of this table is available online at www.SandyAnastasi.com.

Chapter 2

Radionics and the Art of Using a Pendulum

People have been using pendulums for thousands of years. They are among the oldest of the many divination tools in use today. Although there are many fine and beautiful pendulums available, technically any object that hangs freely on a string, wire, or chain can be used as a pendulum. There are pendulums made of crystal, of metal, of precious and semi precious stones, and of wood (Barbara Brennan, author of *Hands of Light*, recommends wooden pendulums in her book for dowsing the aura for illness). I've even seen them made of plastic, which I don't particularly like because plastic does not retain an energy charge well, so these are actually more difficult to use. Perhaps the best pendulum for a beginner is some article of jewelry that you have worn often enough to charge with your own energy, and that can be easily attached to a string or chain. To be used as a pendulum it must swing freely, not be too long, and it should be fairly narrow or come to a point when you are looking down at it so that you can see what it is pointing at. Because it already feels like you, you will be likely to get it to work for you more quickly than a fancy pendulum you purchased.

My favorite pendulums are of stone or metal, swing freely, and are on a string or chain that is about 6 to 8 inches long, or a bit longer if you want to wrap one end around your finger when you're using it. I've even made a pendulum from a plumb bob once or twice. These I liked since the top unscrews and you can put a bit of an herb to enhance divination (wormwood) or a small piece of crystal inside. The only problem with these is that they are apt to be a bit heavy. I have seen similar pendulums that opened for sale though, too, if you want something lighter, but they are also more expensive.

Pendulums have been used to tell the sex of a child, to answer questions, to locate objects, and more recently, in Radionics to test an energy field. This latter use is much like dowsing, which I will also briefly discuss in this chapter.

When I first began to experiment with pendulums, there were no books on the subject, so my own traditional pendulum knowledge is entirely self-taught. When I first began using a pendulum for divination, the field of Radionics was not yet developed. Later on when I learned about Radionics, I found an entirely different way of using pendulums, which fit an entirely different area of usage. So, I began to teach both techniques. My own is how to use a pendulum for divination – to answer a yes or no question or to locate something; it is the more traditional approach. Radionics on the other hand is similar to muscle testing or, as it is otherwise known in the metaphysical field,

Kinesiology. In Radiology the pendulum is hung in the energy field of a person or object, and the motion of the pendulum tells you what you want to know about them. In this chapter you will learn both techniques since both are valid and can be employed in entirely different ways.

When you use a pendulum in the more traditional fashion, for divination, it is necessary to protect yourself completely because in asking questions of the pendulum you are opening yourself to forces and perhaps entities outside of yourself. Because of this, I will be teaching you a very strong method of protection that you should always employ before using ANY method of divination where you open to any force outside of YOU. That includes getting information from your guides, whom we will meet via a guided visualization presented a little later on in the chapter.

When you use a pendulum for Radionics this protection is not necessary because you are not opening to anything outside of yourself. Since the Radionics application of the pendulum is safer, let's start with that.

The Radionics Approach to Using a Pendulum

First, purchase a pendulum, or select an item of your jewelry that tapers to a point and hang it from a string or single chain (not looped – that will impede its motion) that is about 6 to 8 inches long.

Next, hold the pendulum by the string in your dominant hand, placing your other hand palm up beneath it. Just relax, as you deepen your breathing and allow the energy to flow into, through, and out both hands.

Momentarily the pendulum will begin to move, gradually tracing a circle over your upheld palm. The circle may be either clockwise or counter clockwise; whatever it is, that will be a 'yes' answer to any question you ask over the next two hours. A spin in the opposite direction will be a 'no' answer during this same time period.

This is because the body's polarity shifts every two hours, so in two hours you will need to repeat the process to double check which direction will be a yes and which a no. Note that yes and no answers using Radionics do not come from an outside source; they come from a direct reading of the energy you are testing. You'll read more about that on the following pages.

Meanwhile, Figure 2 shows you how to find the direction of spin.

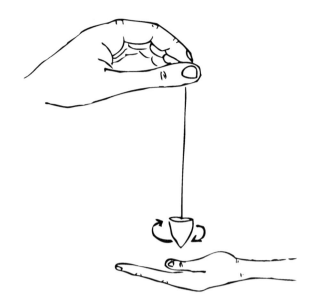

Figure 2: Establishing the Direction of Spin for a Yes or No Answer Using Radionics

Now you are ready to apply the principles of Radionics using a pendulum to test the flow of energy in an aura, the direction of energy flow and openness of the chakras, and even whether a food or drug item is good for you!

Food Testing

Let's start by testing if a particular food is good for you. Why not start with sugar? Go get some sugar (a packet is fine, or you can just set the sugar bowl in front of you). Now you are ready (having already checked out which direction of spin is 'yes' and which 'no' right now) to hold your pendulum over the sugar, essentially in its energy field, and ask, "Is this good for me to eat right now?"

But some of you reading this will undoubtedly be saying to yourself, this whole thing is absurd. Anyone can make a pendulum move however he or she wants it to.

This, of course, is true. The trick is to hold your hand steady by bracing your elbow on a solid stable surface while holding the string or chain firmly between your index finger and thumb. The object you will test is placed beneath the pendulum. You plan for as little motion of your own as possible.

However, you will still be causing the pendulum to move with the tiny muscles in your fingertips. The muscle movement is unconscious, not deliberate. And that is exactly what you want. You see, as you hold the pendulum in the aura or energy field of the object you are testing, your unconscious mind registers the energy of the object and gives you an accurate assessment, which transmits to those muscles in your fingertips and from there to moving the pendulum in a yes or no circle.

So let's get back to the sugar. You have your elbow resting on the table, the pendulum is being held firmly in your dominant hand, you've already tested for which direction of spin is 'yes' or 'no' for the moment, and you are holding the pendulum over the sugar. In your mind you hold the thought, "Is this good for me right now?"

Again, note that you must hold that thought in your mind with focus. If your mind strays while you are doing the testing, you will end up testing for something else. Energy follows thought.

Most of you who just tested that sugar would have found that it is NOT good for you (sugar is by and large not good for anyone). However, if you are low on energy at the moment, you might have received a 'yes' answer because sugar is an energy food.

And now go get some of the foods you KNOW are not good for you, and try the same thing on them. And get some foods that ARE good for you and try it on those, too. Substantiate your findings. Prove to yourself this works. And when you get really good at this, carry your pendulum with you to the grocery store as some people do, and you will be able to find out if fruit has been waxed or sprayed (just hold the thought in your mind as you hold the pendulum over it), if meat is fresh, or if a particular food is good for you or not.

If you are standing when you do the testing you can use your other hand to brace your elbow, or if you feel you are steady enough, just hold the pendulum directly over the object you are testing, without bracing.

Now try the same thing on the medications you have in your medicine cabinet. Ask if a certain medication would be good for something it was not originally purchased for, then check out your answer to ascertain its accuracy.

The next time you are ill you can experiment on yourself. Go to the medicine cabinet and dowse with your pendulum to see which medicine it says will be the best for curing whatever is ailing you. (Remember, this is no substitute for going to the doctor if you are REALLY sick!) Then, before you use it, read the packaging or check it out in a medical book unless you already know it is meant for whatever is ailing you. This will supply valuable feedback and reinforcement for you.

Mixing an aromatherapy oil? Hold the purpose you want to achieve steady in your mind, and dowse the essential oils you have available to see which will serve that purpose. Now that you have your oils selected, dowse again to determine how much of each oil to use. To do this, just write the amounts down on a piece of paper, and use the figures where you get a yes.

The above examples are the most common ways that people use Radionics. But it can also be used to dowse the aura around a person for illness, or to dowse the chakras to see if they are open and to determine their direction of spin. Let's see how these techniques are done. Many people in the holistic medical field today are using pendulums to dowse in this manner to determine areas of illness, as well as treatments. Although I encourage you to investigate and practice this, please remember to always consult a health professional for confirmation of your findings.

Dowsing the Aura for Health

This application of Radionics is not very different than your food testing. But in this case, you will be working with a person (you can do this on animals and plants, too, but for now stick to people because from them you can get feedback).

First, you need to focus your mind on what you are looking for. Once you are focused, the pendulum will only become active (moving in a 'yes' circle) if the illness you focused on is present in an area. If it is not, it will remain still.

Try it first on a friend or partner looking for areas of stress or tension. Since most people have some of these areas this is a good thing to dowse for even in a healthy young person. Mentally focus your thoughts so that you are looking for points of stress or tension.

Now, if you are short, you may have your partner sit in a chair that is open in back, or on a stool. If you are tall have him (or her) stand.

Start by holding the pendulum in his aura above his head. Gradually bring the pendulum down and around him, checking each part of his body slowly. You can move clockwise or counterclockwise around, but move gradually from head to toe in each area you cover, all the while holding in your mind that you are looking for places where stress and tension have accumulated.

Each time the pendulum begins to circle 'yes' tell your partner what area it is, and get his feedback.

If occasionally the pendulum moves in a 'no' direction it probably means that this is a place he would normally carry stress, but right now he has none.

When you are done looking for stress points, go back and dowse to see if your partner has any physical problem that might need medical attention. Follow the same pattern, but hold this new thought in your mind. Do you see that the pendulum circles 'yes' in different places than it did before? Or perhaps if your partner is healthy, it doesn't move at all!

Get feedback from your partner. If you found areas needing medical attention, what is the complaint? Is he receiving treatment?

If your partner indeed has a medical problem and is receiving treatment or is on some form of medication, have him write the type of treatment or medication down on a piece of paper and dowse it as you would a food or drug item to determine if it is the right thing to use for his medical condition.

So you see merely by writing down the name of something you can call enough of its vibrational energy in to dowse it using Radionics.

Next we are going to see how the Radionics method of using a pendulum can be used to determine the directional flow of the chakras, as well as whether a chakra is open or closed. This is an especially valuable tool because, as you will see, it can readily be used for biofeedback as well, helping you to open the chakras by concentrating on them, and also allowing you to adjust the direction and amount of energy flowing in and out of each one. This is especially important for people who are studying to become professional psychics because one of the major hazards professional psychics face is their tendency to shut down the lower psychic energy centers, or chakras, which ultimately leads to ill health. Using the pendulum, you can dowse to see if the centers are open, and even learn to consciously open and close them readily because the pendulum will let them know if they are successfully doing it or not.

Dowsing the Chakras Using Radionics

In this technique we will not be looking at the direction of spin of the pendulum as a yes or no answer, but rather as an indication of which way the chakra itself is spinning.

If the pendulum spins clockwise in front or over a chakra, it will tell you that the chakra is at the moment pulling energy from spirit into matter, and grounding it. It is taking energy in. If the pendulum spins counterclockwise in front or over a chakra, it means that the chakra is bringing energy from matter into spirit – it is putting energy from the person out into the world around him or her.

Now, your chakras may change their direction of spin every two hours (or not) as the polarity of the body shifts. Also, I have read in many books that the chakras are 'supposed' to spin in alternating directions. I personally have not found this to be the case. I have seen many people where five out of seven chakras were all spinning the same direction, and these people were not unhealthy in any way. So much for alternating directions. From my experience, the direction of spin merely tells you which way the energy is flowing. Is the person pulling it in (clockwise) or putting it out (counterclockwise)?

Of more importance than the direction of spin is whether energy is flowing in or out of the chakra at all, and if so, at what rate.

If you hold the pendulum over or in front of a chakra and it does not move it will tell you that chakra is closed. But with focus, the person can open it. What he must do is focus on the chakra, and as he does, he will bring energy to it. Remember, energy follows thought. The more the person focuses on that chakra, the more energy will flow through it. You will see the pendulum begin to make tiny circles, which will gradually get bigger and faster as the chakra opens to pull more energy through it.

Now, to start your chakra dowsing, hold your pendulum over your partner's Crown Center, at the top of his head, first. Remember, direction of spin tells you if energy is going in (clockwise) or coming out (counter clockwise) and the size and speed of the circle the pendulum makes tells you if the chakra is open, and how open.

Next, move to the Throat Center, holding your pendulum in front of your partner's throat area, and do the same thing.

Move down to the Heart Center, holding the pendulum in front of your partner's chest, and check the spin direction and size there.

Now, in turn, check the Solar Plexus Center, located at the base of the sternum, the Sacral Center, two inches below the navel, and the Root Center, at the groin area, holding the pendulum in front of each center in turn and noting its direction of spin, and the size and speed of the spin.

As you do this, allow your partner to take the time to focus on each chakra that is closed or has a small spin, so that he can use this biofeedback opportunity to open the center and improve the rate of energy flow through it.

If he is unable to get it completely open at this time, tell him to not worry about it, repeated work with the pendulum and his own concentration will eventually get it to where it needs to be.

Of course, it is also nice to know that armed with a full-length mirror in your home you can also dowse your own chakras and even dowse yourself for health problems, provided you can keep your attention focused and keep your mind from wandering and over-focusing on possible fear issues. Testing the chakras though is the best use of this though because you really can use the pendulum for yourself, as a biofeedback tool to open and develop all of the chakras to their fullest potential.

Try this experiment: Do the Chakra Exercise from Psychic Development Level 1, bringing energy into each chakra, starting with the Root Center and eventually pushing it out through the Crown Center. When you have completed the exercise, stand in front of your mirror and dowse each of your psychic energy centers to see the direction and rate of spin. Or if a friend is available, have him or her use the pendulum to do the dowsing.

For those of you who are having trouble recalling where the chakras are, the following diagram, repeated from Psychic Development Level 1, will help:

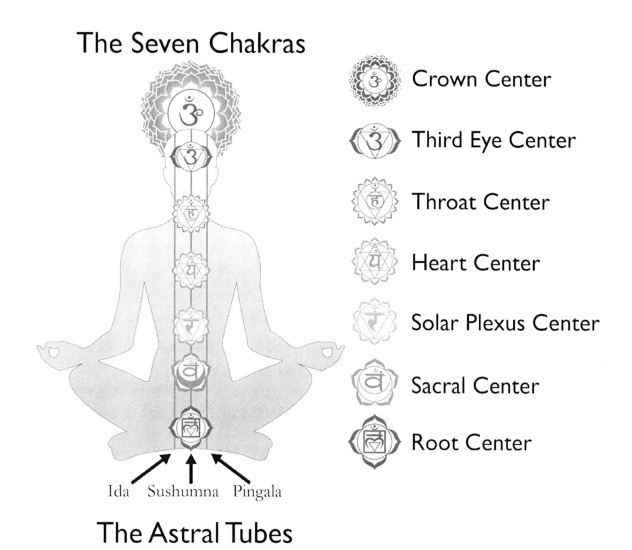

Figure 3: The Seven Chakras

Before we move on to the more traditional uses of the pendulum in divination, I have just a few more words to say on dowsing.

In the last chapter, when you did the exercise of spinning around slowly, hands outstretched, to find the best direction for your psychic work, you were already doing a form of dowsing. Many people who are energy sensitive have natural dowsing ability.

It is most common to see professional dowsers looking for water. Professional water dowsers usually work with two dowsing rods, traditionally made of wood, but more recently made of various types of metals. In areas where water is hard to find, or lies beneath the surface but is only shallow enough for a well to reach to in certain areas, people will call in a dowser to locate that one place they can dig their well and reach water. This is an old and well-respected profession because it works! Usually the dowser makes a grid out of the yard or place he is to dowse, and then he walks the grid, a dowsing rod in either hand, just allowing himself to be sensitive to the pull he feels on the tips of the rods as he focuses on finding water. Sure enough, when he gets to the spot the water is close to the surface, the rods tip down, usually in unison. It is amazingly effective! And the same technique can be applied to finding other things, too.

I'm sure you can see the similarity to dowsing with the pendulum. Trying it with dowsing rods is equally gratifying. Incidentally, you can also use the dowsing rods to measure the size of the aura. The person with the dowsing rods stands 20 or 30 feet away from the person whose psychic aura is being measured, and gradually walks closer, dowsing rods extended, until all of a sudden the rods will drop and cross, which means you are at the edge of the aura. Try measuring an aura with dowsing rods, then doing the Chakra Exercise, and then measuring it again! It's a wonderful before-and-after test. Dowsing rods may be purchased through any New Age store, or made from to lightweight wooden or metal rods. They usually have some sort of handle or elbow to hold on one end.

Using a Pendulum for Divination

For thousands of years people have been using pendulums as a means of psychically divinating answers to their most pressing questions.

When a pendulum is used in this fashion it requires that you open up psychically to get your answers from a source outside of yourself – unless you limit your focus to communication only with your Higher Self, which is safer, and which some people do. You are yourself perfectly capable of doing that right now, having learned already how to make a strong connection to your Higher Self.

First, before you say, "Oh, that's absurd... I've played with a pendulum before on my own, asking questions, and nothing bad happened!" please remember that that was before you'd done all this work to open yourself psychically. For the most part, the average person is not capable of really opening up to those outside energies and entities widely enough to draw something in that could harm him or her. By now, if you've studied the materials in Psychic Development Levels 1 and 2, you are. You are no longer average!

Using a pendulum for divination purposes is much like working with a Ouija board (discussed in Chapter 5 of this book), which I also caution against doing at this point, unless fully protected. I am sure you have already heard all of the horror stories about Ouija boards and possession... and they are not far from the truth. The same potential pitfalls lie before you when using a pendulum for divination, if to a slightly lesser extent.

So, to guard against this, before I even teach you my method of using a pendulum for divination, I will teach you to thoroughly protect yourself. This protection is so effective that I assure you if you employ it any time you do psychic divination work of any kind you will never draw any harm to yourself.

It involves a series of steps, one of which is to contact and bring in your guides, first your *Protector* and then your *Life Guide*. So, before you can learn the protective technique I use, you will have to meet these guides.

Even if you think you know some of your guides, and have been working with them for years, please do the following exercise. It arranges for you to meet, while in a protected space, the particular guides you will need for your divination work, who have been with you all of your life. Many people who have been seeing or otherwise getting information from guides and angels (for most people the term *angel* is interchangeable with *guide*) all of their lives may actually see the same guides they are used to dealing with. But others may be surprised that the guides they are introduced to in this exercise are beings they have never consciously met before, though they have been with them all along.

I believe that all of us come into life with two main guides that are with us all of our lives; these are our Life Guide and our Protector. It is as if, before birth, we made a pact with these guides that they would be there to help us on our way whenever we listened for them. Your Life Guide is the guide that is there to help you to move in the right direction to meet your life goals, whatever they may be. In your psychic divination work your Life Guide will act much as what many psychic mediums call a *control* or *gatekeeper*. Your Life Guide will be the guide you get your actual information from, though that guide may sometimes consult with others to provide you with that information. Your Protector is the guide that will actively block away from you any negative forces or entities while you are doing any divination work.

In the following guided visualization exercise you will not only meet both of these important guides, you will also learn how to contact them to ask for their help whenever you need to invoke their presence.

Of course, you have many other guides as well. If you are interested in learning about them and meeting them, you can do so by taking my class on *Seeing Beyond the Veil*; it is available on both audio and videotape, and will soon be available in paperback and eBook formats as well.

I am including two variations on the Meeting Your Guides Exercise here. The first is the one I originally taught my students, the second is a variation developed by John Maerz. You are sure to find one of them effective.

If you are someone who does guided visualizations more readily by listening to them, I suggest you either have a friend read the exercise to you, or put it on an audiotape yourself, and lie back and just go with it. If you like, you may also purchase the meditations in this book on CD from my Web site. For those of you who are good at visualizing while reading, it will be fine to do just read the exercise to yourself, visualizing each part as you go. Following the exercise, write down everything you saw, felt, or heard... write down ALL of your impressions. The exercises begin on the following page.

Exercise #1: Meeting Your Guides, Technique 1

1. Close your eyes. Take three deep diaphragmatic breaths to ground and center.

2. Use your 10-point progressive relaxation or other exercise to enter a state of body asleep – mind awake. The 10-point relaxation was given in Psychic Development Level 1.

3. When you have completed the 10-point relaxation, continue to breathe deeply and rhythmically as you allow yourself to enter a meditative state for a few minutes as you focus only on your breath.

4. Now, move from your meditation with focus on the breath to imagine yourself walking along a perfect white beach. You feel the sand beneath your feet, smell the salt air, and hear the cry of sea gulls.

5. You begin to follow a path that leads inland away from the strand of beach, toward your workplace.

6. Outside the door of your workplace is your worry box.

7. In your mind's eye take your worry box and put into it all of your cares and concerns – anything that might get in the way of the exercise. Even put your

physical body in there if you like so it will not be a distraction either. Now close the lid on the worry box. Leave it outside the door.

8. Next move into to your magical workplace on the inner planes. As you go through the door look all around, a full 360 degrees, to see if anything new has been added since you were last here. Or if this is the first time you are visualizing your workplace, make a note of what it looks like.

9. In the center of your workplace is a worktable. On the table is your energy screen, which you can stand on the floor and enlarge until it is as big as a doorway. Do this now.

10. Now, step through the doorway into a long hallway. This hall has doors on either side that for the moment, you will ignore. You need to travel all the way down this hall, but you cannot yet see the end – it just seems to go on and on. You begin to walk down it, then you are running, and before long you are flying. The doors to either side are moving by you faster and faster. Everything around you starts to spin as your speed intensifies, until finally you see double doors straight ahead of you. As you approach, the doors open up into utter darkness or incredible brilliance.

11. Look outward into the light and extend your left hand into it. Mentally ask for your Protector guide. Feel a hand grasp your own. Look at the hand holding yours. Is it large or small, male or female; is it strong? Now let your gaze travel up your Protector's arm. Is your Protector wearing anything on the arm? Is it muscular or slender? Continue looking up to his (or her) shoulders, and then his face. What does he look like? Look at his eyes. The eyes are the windows of the soul. What do your Protector's eyes say to you?

12. Now ask your Protector his (or her) name. Ask for his help. Ask how you may best call him to you. You will hear these answers in your mind. Don't think about it or let your conscious mind get in the way… just accept the first words you hear.

13. Now give your Protector your thanks.

14. Next, look outward into the light again and extend your right hand into it. Ask for your Life Guide to meet you. Feel the hand of your Life Guide grasp yours. Again, look at the hand that is holding yours. Is it old or young, male or female? Gentle or strong? Slowly move your gaze up his (or her) arm. Note what, if anything, he is wearing. Now look at his face, and his eyes. As you make eye contact ask your Life Guide's name, or the name that you can call him by. Ask for his help and information, and how you may best call him to you. Again, you will hear the answers in your mind.

15. Now give your Life Guide your thanks, too.

16. Now, turn from this place, and travel back down the hall. Again, the doors to the sides flash by as you are enveloped by a sensation of speed and spinning.

17. Finally, you step back through the doorway that is your energy screen into your workplace. As you look about you to see what has changed or been added (changes here always represent changes in yourself) you might be surprised to find your guides here. Only they and you can enter this place. It is your own safe, private place on the inner planes.

18. Last, count yourself awake, starting with 10 and counting slowly back to 1, normal waking consciousness. Open your eyes.

Exercise #2, following, is a variation developed by John Maerz. Try it and use the variation that proves most effective for you.

Exercise #2: Meeting Your Guides, Technique 2

---

1. Close your eyes. Take three deep diaphragmatic breaths to ground and center.

2. Use your 10-point progressive relaxation or other exercise to enter a state of body asleep – mind awake. The 10-point relaxation was given in Psychic Development Level 1.

3. Now picture a point of white light in the center of your chest and gradually expand it outward, powering it with the breath, expanding it outward on each exhalation.

4. At the same time, imagine yourself surrounded in brilliant white light, drawing it into yourself on each inhalation, until the white light outside you merges with the white light inside you.

5. In your mind's eye take out your worry box and put into it all of your cares and concerns – anything that might get in the way of the exercise. Even put your physical body in it if you like so it will not be a distraction either. Now close the lid on the worry box and slide it around behind you where you cannot see it.

6. Next, move to your magical workplace on the inner planes. As you go through the door look all around, a full 360 degrees, to see if anything new has been added since you were last here. Or if this is the first time you are visualizing your workplace, make a note of what it looks like.

7. In your workplace is a spiral staircase that goes upward. Begin to climb up the stairway; pass the first floor you come to an area that houses your control room. Continue to climb up, and up, until you come to the next floor that is filled with brilliant white light.

8. Look outward into the light and extend your left hand into it. Mentally ask for your Protector. Feel a hand grasp your own. Look at the hand holding yours. Is it large or small, male or female. Is it strong? Now let your gaze travel up your Protector's arm. Is he (or she) wearing anything on the arm? Is it muscular or slender? Continue looking up to his shoulders, and then his face. What does he look like? Look at his eyes. The eyes are the windows of the soul. What do your Protector's eyes say to you?

9. Now ask your Protector his name. Ask for his help. Ask how you may best call him to you.

10. Now give your Protector your thanks.

11. Next, look outward into the light again and extend your right hand into it. Ask for your Life Guide to meet you. Feel the hand of your Life Guide grasp yours. Again, look at the hand that is holding yours. Is it old or young, male or female? Gentle or strong? Slowly move your gaze up his (or her) arm. Note what, if anything, he is wearing. Now look at his face, and his eyes. As you make eye contact ask your Life Guide's name, or the name by which to call him. Ask for his help and information, and how you may best call him to you.

12. Now give your Life Guide your thanks, too.

13. Finally, walk back down the spiral staircase. Your guides may or may not come with you. Pass the floor with the control room, and return to your main workplace. As you look about you to see what has changed or been added (changes here always represent changes in yourself) you might be surprised to find your guides here.

14. Last, count yourself awake, starting with 10 and counting slowly back to 1, normal waking consciousness. Open your eyes.

In doing the above exercises, you were unable to get your guides names, or were unable to see them clearly, don't feel badly. It will come in time. The important thing is that you got enough of a feel for them that you can call them back again by mentally replaying the part, for example, of reaching out and holding each of their hands.

And if you are one of those people, I commiserate. It was many years before I was able to know whom my guides were for sure, and even longer than that before I learned their names!

Right from the beginning I had been seeing them in my dreams, but never identified them as guides because they looked and dressed like normal people. It wasn't until much, much later that I happened upon them in the robes of a spiritual order, and realized that not only were they not normal people, not only did they belong to some sort of order on the other planes, but they actually knew each other. Then I learned that they didn't just guide me... in my case I share my guides with countless other people on the planet.

And it was still years before I learned their names. In fact, in for many years I was teaching my students to meet their guides, and my students were receiving their guides' names, and I still didn't know mine. My guides finally led me to real world representations of themselves so that I could learn who they were!

Also, be aware that your guides have probably lived many lifetimes, just as you have. The names your guides gave you may have been the names you knew them by in another lifetime, or it may even just be names that are a good link for you to call them in, not really their actual names at all. But it will be the names they go by for you.

Now that you have met your guides, you are ready to learn the protection technique that I would like you to use prior to doing all divination work, or whenever you are opening psychically to something outside of yourself.

Exercise #3: Psychic Protection for Divination Work

1. Close your eyes and take three deep diaphragmatic breaths to ground and center.

2. Surround yourself in white light. Use whatever technique works best for you.

3. Put yourself in your energy balloon that you learned in Psychic Development Level 1. By now, if you've been working with this you have gotten to the point where you can do this with three more deep breaths accompanied by a visualization. If you need a review, I've included one following this exercise.

4. Say a prayer of protection. If you have a personal prayer that you have already been using, use it... it will have personal meaning to you. I will share with you the one that I use, which I have found to be very effective both in adding protection, as well as opening to higher forces. Here it is:

    a. "In the name of all that is..."

    b. "I heal, cleanse, and protect my mind, my body, and my spirit"

    c. "In the name of all that is..."

    d. "I ask to be a channel for the universal force."

5. Now, invoke your guides. If they gave you their names, ask for them to come and help you in your work by name... first calling in your Protector, then your Life Guide. If you received no names, then recall the feeling of grasping their hand, or visualize them... again, bring in your Protector first, then your Life Guide.

a. If your guides tell you no, shake their heads 'no' or give you any feeling that they do not want to help you in the particular work you are doing, it is their way of telling you that they do not want you to do this. So DON'T. If you don't listen to them, they will not make themselves available to help and protect you.

6. Now you are fully protected, so you may open your eyes and do your psychic divination work. As you do your work, it will be your Higher Self and your Life Guide that you are asking your questions of. Don't forget to follow the rest of the steps below when you are done.

7. When your divination work is completed, close your eyes and visualize both of your guides, or say their names to yourself. Thank them for helping you with your work, then let them go.

8. Breathe your energy balloon back into yourself and then exhale the balloon back into the universe, letting it go.

*If you have forgotten the energy balloon from Psychic Development Level 1, here it is again:

1. Close your eyes. Now, holding the white light around you, focus on that part of it that is beneath your feet. Feel your feet get warm and tingle as you focus on the light. You will do this next part three times. The first time let the light enter the soles of your feet, and feel the tingling spread up your body, as you inhale, and pull the light all the way up to the top of your head with your inhalation. When it gets to the top of your head, let it sprout out of your crown like a fountain, and spray down all around you. When it gets down to your feet, curl the light around to re-enter them, creating a balloon of light. The second time there is a variation – pull the light up through your feet again using your inhalation, but as it enters your feet, spin the white light counterclockwise – that is toward your left, as you breathe it up to the crown of your head, and when you fountain it out, let it burst from the top of your head as blue light swirling down and around you in a clockwise direction (toward your right) as you exhale. The third time do exactly the same thing as the second. Now you are in a protective blue energy balloon that is spinning clockwise around you.

2. To release it, when you sprout it out the top of your head see it go out into the universe, instead of around you to form the balloon.

Asking Yes and No Questions

The simplest and fastest way to use your pendulum for divination is to ask yes or no questions, addressing these questions to your Higher Self or your Life Guide.

Please be aware though, that the principle of garbage-in-garbage-out often joked about in the computer world also applies here. Your answer will only be as accurate and as concise as your question is. And if you keep asking the same question over and over again, your guides either stop answering entirely, or start to give you answers to something different, since they can't believe you are so foolish that you would want to keep hearing the same answer! Many people do poorly with the pendulum when it is used in this manner for that reason.

Also, note that you should never try to ask emotionally charged questions. It is usually when you are overly emotional about something that you run for the pendulum to ask your guides what the outcome of your dilemma will be; and unfortunately for most people the extreme emotion they are experiencing will block the channel that your guides use to communicate, so you get shaky information at best... even if your guides do manage to get the answer through, if it's an answer you don't like, you will usually keep trying to change it to what you want to hear. I think I have made my point! You should really use your pendulum for questions about things that you are not emotionally vested in. If you have a very emotional question to ask, I suggest you ask it of a friend who also does divination.

When you are using your pendulum for divination, you may use the circular patterns for yes and no that you learned earlier in the chapter, or you may use the method that I have used for years, that I arrived at by trial and error.

It is really simple. If the pendulum swings toward me and away from me (as if it's following my nose as I shake my head 'yes') it is a yes. If it swings left and right (as if I'm shaking my head 'no') it is no. If it swings in a circle it means 'I don't know' or 'this question isn't clear.'

I like to use this technique when I'm using a pendulum for divination because it gives you that third, 'I don't know' or 'this question isn't clear' option.

Also, when using this method, the pendulum motion will always be the same for a yes, no, or I-don't-know answer. It does not have to be re-tested each time you use it.

To give you an idea of how to phrase questions when you work with your pendulum, I've written some bad questions below, and their good question counterparts:

1. Will I sell my house? (Bad question. Of course you will probably sell it *someday*!)

    a. Reworded good question – Will I sell my house in three months?

2. Will I get a raise and a new position? (Bad question. You are asking two questions at the same time. Break them down to two separate questions, and add a time period to increase accuracy.)

a. Reworded good questions – Will I get a new position this year? Will I get a raise with it if I do?

3. Will my mother like my new boyfriend? (Bad question. The question is too broad. There will undoubtedly be things she likes about him, and things she doesn't.)

   a. Reworded good question – Will my mother get along with my new boyfriend? – it's probably what you would really have meant in the first place!

Don't forget to write your questions down, and to date them. Beneath them write the answers that you get. Leave space to write down eventual confirmation, as you receive it. This will give you a record of questions and answers that you will gradually be able to use to improve the level of communication between you and your guide so that you gradually get more and more accurate information.

I have found over the years that I like to use the pendulum most for these simple yes or no questions, or for mapping or time divination, which I'll discuss a bit later on. Many of you reading this though want to get more information while using your pendulum, which entails using it much like a Ouija board, even though it is very slow going to use the pendulum in this manner (just as it is slow going to use a Ouija board!)

However, if you are patient, and fully protected, this can be done safely.

Using a Pendulum Like a Ouija Board

What you will need to do is to make a sort of 'Ouija board' yourself, on a piece of paper. You can use an 8-1/2"x11" sheet. Set it up similar to this, but with even more space around each number or letter:

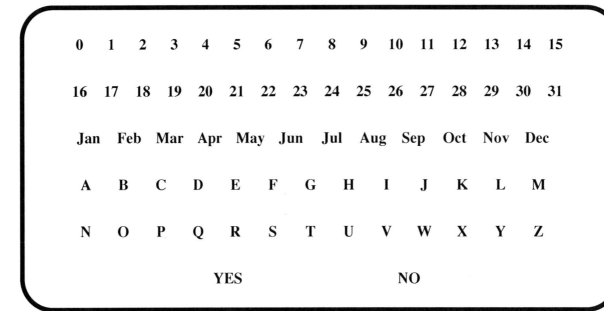

Figure 4: A Ouija Board

Now, before proceeding, go back to the Exercise #3 and do your protection. When you are done, think about a question you have that requires more than a yes or no answer. Write it down and date the paper.

To get your answer, rest your elbow on a table and dangle the pendulum from your relaxed hand, holding the end firmly between thumb and forefinger. Now, move the paper beneath the pendulum number by number, letter by letter, holding the question in your mind all the time, until the pendulum begins to circle over one of the digits. That is your first letter. Now, move onto your second, third, etc., until you have spelled out a word, a date, or even a whole sentence. This is very slow going, but some people like getting more information than the simple yes or no technique I described earlier.

When you are finished, write down the information you received and release your protection.

Mapping: Using a Pendulum to Locate Someone or Something

The practice of using a pendulum becomes a fine art when it is used for locating a person, or an item, that has been lost, or locating things for other reasons as well. This is not only fun, it is immensely satisfying. However, it is not easy.

One of the problems with lost people, or animals, is that they tend to move. So there you are, holding your pendulum over a map of the area in which the dog was lost, for example (while fully protected), and slowly moving the map beneath the pendulum just as we did when using the pendulum like a Ouija board; your pendulum begins to wildly circle right over the juncture of Walnut St. and Pine St. So you get in your car and race to the intersection only to find the dog was seen there 15 minutes ago, and could be anywhere in a 15-minute radius run at top speed right now!

You see, both people and animals tend to move. So although your divination of where they are may be accurate, unless you ask your question VERY intelligently, you will not be able to locate them with the pendulum. In the above example (which actually happened to me, I might add) if I had asked where the dog would be, say, one hour from now, I might well have found it there! As it was, I tracked it all over the area, and finally followed it home, but never did actually find it! The same thing, of course, is true of people.

Another brief comment about locating people: Give some thought to the fact that sometimes people don't want to be found. I remember helping an adopted girl find her natural mother once - with dire consequences. The mother did not want her. So, weigh each situation separately, and if your gut says, "Don't do this one," then don't.

Finding something that is lost also presents problems that can sometimes be eliminated with careful wording. For example, a question of, "Where is my lost earring?" could lead you on a wild goose chase if you drew a map of your home, assuming the earring was lost there, and it wasn't. Better to narrow it down with yes and no questions – i.e., "Is my lost earring in my home?" before starting to look for it there. If you are looking for a lost object, you can narrow the search down with questions to a specific place and room, sometimes even specific furniture. Or, you can create a site-map. In that case, you hold the pendulum still as we did above, moving the map beneath it. In a site-map where you are looking for a specific item, or a specific place that it would be good to do something in, as we will do in our End Of Chapter Exercise, it is important to create a floor plan of the house or other building in which you are looking for the item, and put in all the key pieces of furniture, too.

Storing and Caring for Your Pendulum

A pendulum used for divination is a very personal item. It becomes, over time, an extension of you. Therefore, you should keep it away from other people. Others should not handle it or use it. Regardless of what materials your pendulum is made from, it will benefit from being stored in a dark-colored, natural-fiber bag or box. And initially, when you are breaking it in, it is a good idea to carry it on your own person.

End of Chapter Exercise

1. Buy or make yourself a pendulum.

2. Use your pendulum, while fully protected, to ask at least one question a day until you are comfortable working with it.

3. Now, make two site-maps of your home, complete with all of the rooms and furnishings.

   You are going to find two different things; first, the best place in your home to do your divination work, and second, the best place to meditate.

   Hold your pendulum over one of the site-maps of your home. Hold in your mind the focus that you are looking to find the best place in your home to do your divination work in. Move the map under it room by room, until the pendulum begins to circle over one room. Mark that room. Then go on until you have checked out every room, and have marked all of the ones where the pendulum circled. Now, go back over each room checking each place to sit in each room that was a positive. When you are done, you will have several locations in your home where you will achieve good results with your divination.

   Now, repeat the same process, but let your focus be your meditation. You may be surprised to find that your best places to meditate are different than your best places to do divination work. For most people they are. This is because meditation is passive and requires a calm space, whereas for most people divination requires more energy and is more active. You will also find, for both, that the places that were good for you are already your own places, strong with your own vibration.

4. Practice your Radionics on food you are buying or eating, and other things, as often as possible.

5. Do a Radionic Health Scan on someone and get feedback.

6. Check out your own chakras and practice biofeedback with your pendulum to open them daily until you are successful.

7. Continue to record your dreams.

8. Continue to record your psychic impulses.

9. Do a telepathy exercise with your partner – this time try to send a person, a feeling, and a word all together. Don't forget your remote viewing!

Suggested Reading

- *The Science and Art of the Pendulum* by Blackburn
- *The Practical Pendulum Boon* by Jurran

Chapter 3

The Art of Automatic Writing

Automatic writing is one of my favorite and most accurate ways of getting information from my guides and my Higher Self, and I do hope it eventually becomes one of yours as well. Over the years, through automatic writing, I have not only been able to get very accurate future-oriented information on myself and my family, I have also been able to channel information from the higher planes about spiritual issues important to the development of mankind. Much of this information I've been able to use in my teaching and writing. As a matter of fact, for myself, I prefer to use my automatic writing more in this universal fashion, than as a means of receiving personal information. I find that when I receive personal information (especially if it's about something bad) I tend to shut down my Crown Center immediately, which unfortunately puts a stop to other important information I would be getting.

From our guides' point of view, automatic writing is one of the most important tools I teach to my students because it is the tool that allows them to get their message out to people in such a direct way.

There are several different ways of doing automatic writing and I will be presenting them here in this chapter. I will also teach you how to do one method that is perfectly safe and very effective. This is important, because automatic writing is one of the tools that cause you to open wide to your guides, or to whatever else you might invite in! You will be employing the protection you learned in the last chapter when you do this. If you need to you should go back and review it now. The protection technique given in Chapter 2, Exercise #3 is the most important protective technique you will learn. Be sure to memorize it, and always use it when doing your automatic writing or using your other divination tools.

Most of you will elect to use your automatic writing skills for personal or familial information. But there will be some among you who are able to reach further up the planes when writing, who are able to expand your own consciousness to a higher level where you are capable of receiving information with more universal impact. It is for you few that my guides encourage me to teach this skill. You will not need that level of exalted consciousness when getting information for yourself or your client... you only need it if you want to get information with universal impact. Those of you who want to be able to do your automatic writing on this level should be sure to meditate daily, do your Chakra Exercise (learned in Psychic Development Level 1), and do any other spiritual pursuits that work best for you, to become a clear channel and that will allow you to not only reach higher up the planes, but also bring the information you receive down to you with greater clarity.

People like Alice Bailey, who channeled the Tibetan Master Djwal Khul via automatic writing, do their writing from this exalted level of consciousness. They are far and few between; the 'hierarchy' of guides who arduously work to aid the growth and development of mankind are always on the lookout for potential candidates who are willing to do this selfless work. And work it is!

Here's what I'm talking about relative to channeling your automatic writing from various levels:

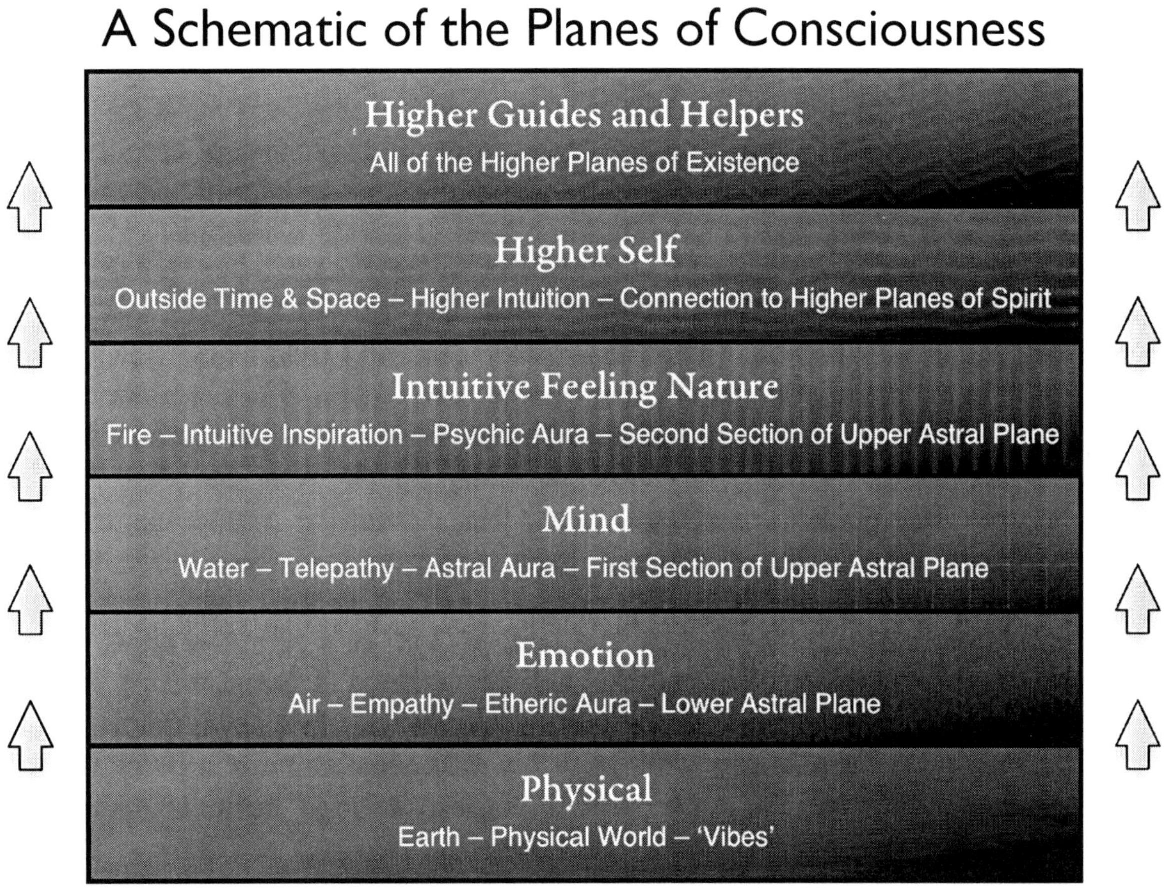

A Schematic of the Planes of Consciousness

Higher Guides and Helpers
All of the Higher Planes of Existence

Higher Self
Outside Time & Space – Higher Intuition – Connection to Higher Planes of Spirit

Intuitive Feeling Nature
Fire – Intuitive Inspiration – Psychic Aura – Second Section of Upper Astral Plane

Mind
Water – Telepathy – Astral Aura – First Section of Upper Astral Plane

Emotion
Air – Empathy – Etheric Aura – Lower Astral Plane

Physical
Earth – Physical World – 'Vibes'

Figure 5: A Schematic of the Planes of Consciousness

From the above schematic, you can see that when you do your automatic writing you are most often working from the plain of *mind* or the plain of *intuitive feeling*... that is the *upper astral plane*. This does require that you raise your consciousness a bit, which will normally occur when you do your protection. When you are channeling from this level you will usually receive information about you and your world in an everyday sense. You do NOT really want to channel your automatic writing from the *lower astral plane*, the plane of emotions, because it is on this level you are most likely to encounter a negative entity or thoughtform... and your guides are not here. When you raise your consciousness way up, to the Higher Self plane or beyond, you will be able to channel information of universal and cosmic import. Now, let's look at the various techniques of doing automatic writing.

The Three Main Methods to Do Automatic Writing

The most common way is actually inspired writing. Many authors of fiction books use this inspired form of automatic writing, much like Jules Verne did, to channel concepts and ideas from their guides and even the *Akasha*. The Akasha, or Akashic Records, is a term used by Edgar Cayce, the famous psychic, to describe the *universal mind*. Carl Jung, noted psychiatrist and metaphysician, described the universal mind as a sort of reservoir of all of mankind's thoughts and ideas from the beginning of creation to the end of creation. Inspired writing allows many authors to access information about past civilizations without having had to fully research it, or gives them the ability to describe devices accurately, that have not yet been invented. In these cases, their guides are not channeling the information directly to them, they are merely sending images and feelings that the writer absorbs, relates to as their own, and then writes down in their own words. It is the concept in these cases that is being given. It is not true automatic writing, which is why I call it inspired writing. The writers get only the concept from the guides, the story line is their own creation. Many people who do what they call 'journaling' from their guides are actually doing this... receiving a basic concept from their guides, and then writing it down in their own words – often, along the way, converting the concept from the guide's original intention to their own interpretation. That interpretation is often presented as 'the word of God,' or a guardian angel or such, and is not. Be wary therefore of so-called channeled writings. If they are truly the result of automatic writing you will get a strong feeling immediately that says, this is the real thing. If they sound like the flowery writings or the religious diatribe of a person making his own point, they are not. They are perhaps inspired writings, but definitely not true automatic writing.

The second type of automatic writing is actually quite dangerous, and though I will describe it, I do not suggest it as a tool for my students. It is doing your automatic writing as a trance channel or trance medium. The trance channel or trance medium goes into trance, a very deep state of mind below the normal alpha level we use in our psychic work (it would be closer to a delta brain wave pattern), and does his (or her) automatic writing from that level of awareness. To him it feels like he is in a state of deep hypnosis, or asleep. But while he is in this state, his hand is busily writing as his guide comes in, takes over, and moves his hand through the automatic writing. When the writing is complete, he wakes up. Although I cannot discount the fact that there are some very good trance channels doing automatic writing, I advise against it since any time we bring a foreign energy, even that of our own guides, into our body it does a little damage to our neural pathways. Ultimately, it can make you very sick, even set the circumstances for an early death. The only exception to this would be if you were channeling your Higher Self, since that is the same energy as you are. Also, if you are essentially asleep while the writing is going on, you have no idea if you may have actually been invaded by a negative entity (this could lead to psychic possession) unless you have really protected yourself very well.

I had an interesting experience with a woman who did automatic writing in trance that I will share with you. I was at an event when she came up to me and asked me my name. When she had ascertained that I was indeed Sandy Anastasi she asked me to meet her in a public parking area on the following day, saying that she did automatic writing and had received a message for me; she knew it was a strange request, but she'd appreciate it if I allowed her to give me the writing. Intrigued, I went the next day to meet her. Sure enough, she was there, waiting with two sheets of paper. One was illegible... it appeared to be a bunch of scratches and dots. The other was clearly written in good penmanship. She explained that she was a trance channel who did automatic writing. She would sit down every day for her writing session at noon, protect, and would go off into a trance and wake up some 15 minutes later with writing in front of her. She said that initially, when she first started this she had only received the pages of gibberish with the scratches and dots. But she continued since it was apparent to her (I don't see how) that it was a language, just not one from our world today. She did her writing daily for some time, but when she never was able to read what she got she eventually asked her guides for a translator. They complied. She began to get the initial information one day from the original guide, and got a translated version the following day from a translator guide. This is one of the strangest methods of automatic writing I have ever come across – but when I looked at the translated sheet it was definitely about me, containing information pertinent to what I was doing at the time. And what is even more interesting is that the original material had been transmitted on my birthday. This total stranger, who would not give me her name, gave me some of the most accurate information I have ever received psychically.

On a different and not so happy note, I had a student many years ago that came to study with me only to learn about automatic writing, not to do it. I only found out her story after she'd completed all my classes, then she told me about her own experience with spirit possession, brought on by unprotected automatic writing. Let me share this with you here. I'm sure she would want you to know, so you do not follow her mistake.

This woman was a gifted writer. She had a dream where she met with men in long robes who appeared very exalted indeed, and who told her that they had information of great importance to dispense to mankind, and that if she was willing, they would like her to be one of the people they gave that information to, to write, because of her skill. Of course she said yes. And upon awaking she decided that she would take it upon herself to learn automatic writing to hasten the process. She wanted them to write THROUGH her, not realizing that when they said they had selected her because of her skill, they were already telling her this was to be inspired writing, they would give the idea but she would organize and present it. But she had already fallen into the first pitfall all psychics who open on this level must struggle to avoid – being led by your ego and vanity. She couldn't wait for them, she had to make it happen NOW. It leaves you wide open to attack from low-level entities every time!

In fact, it is not uncommon for the highest guides to disseminate information via inspired writing because they are so far removed from us and our physical plane that it takes an enormous amount of energy to put information down through the planes into our minds. It is easier for them to send a burst of energy as an idea and let us take it from there, than for them to work directly with us, unless we have learned a method of raising our consciousness up the planes (i.e. – meditation) so that our consciousness is more accessible to them.

But this woman didn't know this, so of course she took it upon herself to learn automatic writing, believing that emissaries of God who wanted her to do this had visited her. (She was also very religious).

So, she got together with a girlfriend who was toying with automatic writing, and learned the basics, unprotected, from her. Then she went home to practice. The first information she received was from a being that gave an angelic name (which actually never existed, by the way) who said that she should not trust him until he could prove he was her real guide. He told her that a friend she had not seen or heard from in five years would call at dinnertime, with a specific reason, that he also gave. Sure enough, at the appointed time, the person called, with that reason. She was hooked. She had proof. He was real, he was an angel, and he was her guide. So, she began to channel automatic writing from him. And right there that should tell you that proof of that nature is not really proof that a being is your guide! Unless YOUR guides that you already met, and know, from Chapter 2 come through themselves, or bring someone through themselves, DO NOT TRUST THAT THE ENTITY IS A GUIDE!

Initially, he gave her information pertinent to her life that reinforced her trust and dependence. She began writing more frequently. Gradually, the real information ceased, only to be replaced by frightening predictions that caused her to enter emotional maelstroms that allowed him to feed off of her energy. This was interspersed with enough real information that she kept coming back for more. She began to write all the time, every chance she could get. She neglected her husband and kids; stopped cleaning, stopped cooking, stopped taking care of herself. Her entire life was in a tailspin that could only end in disaster.

It was lucky for her that she had such a strong religious foundation. One day she felt compelled to go walking, and ended up walking into her church. She was Catholic. She sat down in a rear pew to pray, feeling lost, and hurt. She looked up from her prayers and clairvoyantly saw, for the first and last time in her life, a being that to her was Jesus Christ. And he talked to her briefly. He said, "You are to go home, destroy all of the writings you have received from the false angel, destroy all of your writing implements, and you are to never write again." And he disappeared.

She went home and did exactly as she was told. Between then, and several years later when she studied with me, in order to try to learn and understand what had happened, she had written nothing. She didn't even sign checks any longer. You see, she had become such an open channel for the false angel that any writing implement in her hand was an invitation for it to take over.

Even after taking my classes she never wrote again – even after learning how to protect and how to do automatic writing safely. You see, she had made a promise she wouldn't. And she never did.

The above two stories are real. The second I included not to frighten you, but to show you how serious a matter it is when you do automatic writing to do it properly, and to never do it at all without complete protection. Over the years I have encountered other people who also drew in entities who possessed them in all or in part by using automatic writing improperly, without protection. This is one of the easiest ways a low-level entity, or negative spirit, can invade and take control. Protect, and whatever you do, do not invite it in! You can inadvertently invite such a being in through your fear, or through your needs for ego-fulfillment, which is what happened in this case.

The third form of automatic writing, and what you will be learning in this lesson, is a form where your guide literally guides your hand, without actually entering your body at all. If you are also telepathic you may hear the words as they are written, if you are empathic you will feel what the writing is about… but your guide only guides… doesn't take over. I teach this method to my students because it is as effective as the first two methods, but is far safer.

Here's the technique.

Preparation for Automatic Writing

Be sure to do the complete protection as presented in Exercise #3 of Chapter 2 before you do any automatic writing. Also, if you need to set an alarm clock, do. Automatic writing takes a great deal of energy (YOU supply the energy for the guides to come through) and you won't notice the drain until you're done. Initially set your clock for 15 minutes, and as you gradually get more comfortable with it and it takes less energy to do, you can expand the time until you are up to an hour. Stop there. You don't want to go past that. The best times to do your automatic writing are usually at dawn, dusk, noon, and midnight. Also, any time during the night the air waves are usually quieter, so it is easier to do. You can use your pendulum to determine what the best time(s) and the best place(s) in your house are to do this as well.

Now, you will need to start with an 8-1/2" x 11" sheet of paper, preferably unlined since you are just beginning. Eventually, any paper will do. Also, get a pen or pencil that writes smoothly and easily and is easy to hold on to.

You will also want to begin your writing by asking a question of your guides. That is a sort of door opener. I remember doing this myself as a beginner and just sitting there for an hour with the pen tip on the paper and getting nothing, while my guides were patiently waiting for me to ask them something! I only found that out much later.

And don't forget to date your page, too. This is important because you will probably want to archive your work. Also, some of your writing will be pre-cognitive, and dating it will allow you to see the turn around time on precognitive information received from your guides.

To begin, put the tip of the pen down very lightly on the paper close to the center. Initially, you don't know which direction the writing will come out, so it's important to leave space all around. Brace your elbow on the table as you write, but be sure your hand is able to swing freely. You want the pen to rest lightly because the lighter the pressure the less difficulty your guides (and you) will have moving your hand. Most people, initially, tend to cramp the writing, so you should really attempt to enlarge upon whatever you receive as we do this.

Initially it is a good idea to close your eyes because seeing the writing may distract you into making it happen as opposed to allowing it to happen.

So – you've protected, you've set your alarm clock, you've asked your question and dated your page, and you have placed your pen on the center of the paper. You are ready to begin.

Exercise for Automatic Writing

As you sit with your mind focused on your question, breathing deeply and regularly in a relaxed state, you will begin to feel a sort of pressure on the hand holding the pen, as if it wants to be moved in a certain direction. Go with it. With a light touch, let the pen glide across the paper in that direction, until you feel a directional shift. Then, follow the new direction. Continue to do this until you feel a stop. If the stop is a short one, just lift the pen; you have most likely completed a word. Put the pen back on the paper to start a new word. If it is a long stop, it probably means it is time to start a new line. Occasionally, as you write you will find your pen just making circles... I have found that is my guides' way of saying you are not open enough, your mind is drifting or pre-occupied, clear it and open the channel for us again. I do so by re-centering, refocusing, and taking three deep diaphragmatic breaths as I do this.

As you write your mind may be entirely empty save for the question you are asking, or you may hear the words you are writing as you write them. That is not uncommon. If you do hear them as you write them, take care not to just start writing what you hear. If you do that, your own brain will begin insinuating words and it will no longer be the message from your guides that you are trying to write down.

When you finally open your eyes and look at what you have written, don't be surprised if this first time it looks like gibberish, or if you can only make out one or two words. With practice it will come, and you can get very good at this.

Even if what you've written looks like gibberish, or if you cannot discern any words in it, save it. In time, you may be able to identify what you wrote. I remember myself drawing a shapeless form that I could not recognize, many years before moving to Florida to live. One day when I was looking back through my automatic writing I was surprised to realize that way back then what I had actually drawn was a map of the Florida coastline, complete with an x over the place I would eventually move to!

I also had a student who worked very hard to decipher her automatic writing, which looked like some written language she couldn't recognize (and never did) and finally taught her guide the English alphabet so that she could read the writing! She did this quite easily... just completely protected, as we did above, then showed her guide the alphabet as she thought each letter, and after that it came out in perfect, legible English!

Another student, during class, wrote a set of marks she could not identify. Another student said, "I can read that, it's shorthand!"

So as you can see, it may take you some time to get the hang of it, to get the writing large enough and legible enough to read, and to establish a good communication framework with your guide, but you CAN do this.

Many years ago, while I was doing my automatic writing, my guides asked me why I wanted to do my channeling this way since they were already used to channeling information to me directly. They thought automatic writing was too slow. I answered, "Because this is the way you are the most 'real' to me. When I see the writing coming out, and I KNOW it is not my own thought, my own words, I feel very close to you. I truly know you are there."

That is why, today, I still do automatic writing for myself, though I channel information directly from my guides in every reading for a client that I do.

End of Chapter Exercises

1. Continue recording and interpreting your dreams. Before sleep, rub your Third Eye and ask a question for your guide to give you an answer to in a dream. Ask to wake up immediately following the dream so that you can write it down.

2. Continue recording your psychic experiences.

3. Do a telepathy exercise with a partner: send and receive a simple object, and a word to describe it or enhance it. Don't forget to remote view your partner.

4. Practice your work with psychometry and your pendulum.

5. Practice your newly learned automatic writing skills at least once a day for 15 minutes.

6. Try using breath control with mental projection to control an angry situation. For example, when in line at a store behind an irate customer practice deep, diaphragmatic breathing first to calm yourself, then as you breathe out, extend the calm throughout the vicinity. The irate customer will either calm down, or leave quickly!

Chapter 4

Uncovering What's in Your Unconscious Mind – Initiation!

Facing Your Unconscious Fears

Your unconscious mind is extremely powerful. As a developing psychic, you have been strengthening the functions of that unconscious part of yourself over the entire period of time that you have been studying psychic development. In strengthening it, you have done more than strengthen the psychic abilities you access through it. You have created other positive aspects of it such as its ability to affect your body systems and overall health through your autonomic nervous system. You have also strengthened the negative part of it, the part that is phobic and remains attached to old fears and worries. If you do not do something about that, over time, those fears and worries can become the major focus of your existence.

Childhood Fear Elimination

It is a good idea at this point to learn an important tool for getting to the bottom of your own unconscious fears and worries. There are several reasons why this is important to do.

First, your fears are part of your unconscious mind, which we know is a very powerful projector. This causes us to project our fears into our lives without even realizing we are doing it. But if we don't get a handle on those fears, anxieties, and worries, before long we do find ourselves living them. They undermine our reality, adversely affect our relationships and our health, and lock us into repetitive life actions that prevent our soul growth. So, the first reason to work on identifying, understanding, and releasing our fears is so that we truly eliminate them from having any real impact on our lives.

The second reason is because until we have understood and released our own major fears we are not able to be truly objective in our work with the people we read.

The third reason is that our fears are a point through which negative forces or entities can invade and control us. The more open our psychic work makes us become, the more identifying and releasing our fears becomes a crucial factor. It prevents anything 'not self' from ever getting any kind of hold on us.

And there is another important reason as well... every time we suppress a negative emotion, we also suppress its equal and opposite positive emotion. So, eventually, we are removed from our ability to experience joy, as well as pain.

As we learn to release our fears, we release the very things that have been holding us back from our own growth. The process of bringing the subconscious mind, inclusive of all of its suppressed fears, joys, and life experiences to conscious awareness has been called the process of initiation. It is only by doing work on this that we can become fully conscious beings.

The exercise below is a difficult one to put yourself into fully, but is well worth your time and effort. If you respond well to taped guided visualizations, I suggest you put this one on audiotape and work with it often.

Exercise #1: An Exercise to Uncover and Eliminate Root Causes of Fear

1. Close your eyes. Take three deep diaphragmatic breaths to ground and center.

2. Do your 10-point relaxation exercise.

3. Move to your magical workplace on the inner planes. See what, if anything, has changed there or been added. Changes here reflect changes in you.

4. Move to your worktable, and on it see the worry box into which you have been placing all of your worries, concerns, cares and fears.

5. Go to your worry box, open the lid, and without looking, reach in and grab the first concern that you find. Pull it out to look at it.

6. Identify this thing that is bothering you now. Be totally honest with yourself. With your mind, go over the whole situation until you are perfectly clear about what it is.

7. Now, take another deep, diaphragmatic breath and release it slowly. As you do, look behind this thing you are upset about, back into the past, to the first time you experienced this particular emotion. To do this, totally let go as you breathe out, let an image slowly form in your mind that shows you the situation that existed the first time you felt this particular emotion.

8. Watch the scene as it plays out in your mind. How old are you? Who is involved? What is happening that is making you feel this way? Now, take another deep breath and exhale slowly as you let go of this scene, too…

9. And look behind this emotion, and this scene from your past, to the underlying emotion. For example, if you were jealous, *why* were you jealous? Look at the emotion that underlies and gives rise to the negative emotion you are working to purge.

10. Now look back to the first time you experienced that underlying negative emotion. Look at the situation and the people involved.

11. Be honest with yourself. Accept that you had or have that emotion. Allow yourself in the now to fully feel it. Tell the child within you that it is okay to have that feeling. Accept that child within. Let the child within act out. Let it justify itself. Support it. Let the adult you understand the circumstances that led to your inner child being mistreated in that way, but accept the child and its emotions without reservation. Tell your inner child it was right to feel that way.

12. Now, look again at the scene that contained and gave rise to the underlying emotion, and take a deep breath. As you exhale, breath the scene and the emotions you felt out into the universe where they will be recycled to come back to you in a healthy way.

13. Do the same thing with the situation that was the first time you felt the present negative emotion you are working on.

14. Do the same thing with the present problem.

15. Now hug the child within and reabsorb that little one into you.

16. Turn and look at your workplace. What, if anything, has changed?

17. Count yourself from 10 back to 1, normal waking consciousness. Open your eyes. Write down your experiences.

You will likely never experience that particular negative emotion again, or if you do, it will be in a much less intense form. Congratulations! You have just competed one of the most difficult exercises you will ever do because it requires total self-honesty.

Many of you who did this exercise were surprised by what came out of the worry box; many didn't even remember the situation that had been locked away. That is because children live in the moment, so life is remembered and stored moment by moment. When a child loses memory it can never truly be restored in full because each moment must be remembered separately, unlike adults who remember in a time stream. Yet for most of us, the trapped negative (and equal and opposite positive) emotions originate in childhood. For some, they might even come from a previous lifetime.

I'll share with you my earliest experience with this exercise. To me, at the time, it was devastating. I had a fear of losing a boyfriend I was dating. That is what I pulled out of the worry box. The situation that showed behind that fear showed me as a young child ice-skating with my parents, and my skates were too tight. My feet hurt and I was cold, but I feared to say anything because they might not want me if I caused trouble. When I looked at the scene behind that one, to look at the real underlying emotion, I saw my father tightening the ice skates to where they would cut off the circulation in my feet, and I felt anger. I wasn't dressed warmly enough and I felt anger at my mother as well. I was angry that they would do things to me that hurt, and I couldn't do anything about it. I hated them.

There is no emotion as pure and strong as a child's. The anger and hate I felt in that moment is more intense than any emotion I can ever consciously remember experiencing as an adult. Yet the small child could not say anything, could not release that anger, because of a fear that if she did she would be deserted. I held the child close in my mind and comforted her. I understood my parents' foolishness with my adult mind, but I told my inner child how stupid and foolish those parents were, and she was right, and she had a right to her anger. I told her I loved her and she didn't have to be afraid of desertion. I accepted myself. And in so doing gave myself the right to be angry again, if I so chose; even the right to hate. But I got an unexpected present, too... I gained the ability to love as intensely as I could hate. And I found that I could love my parents again, too.

End of Chapter Exercise

Do the above exercise at least once a week, until you reach a point where confronting your negative emotions is an automatic response, and the underlying causes are clear to you almost immediately.

Chapter 5

The Art of Crystal Gazing or Scrying

Crystal gazing, or *scrying* as it used to be called, is another natural human ability that is easy to learn once you have gone through the basic psychic training given in Psychic Development Level 1. Most people scry quite naturally, never even realizing what they are doing. But when you open to scry you need to use the full protection given in Chapter 2, Exercise #3, because scrying, or crystal gazing is another one of those psychic tools that opens you so wide that you are in danger of invasion by negative energy or a low-level spirit if you do not protect completely.

Also, as hypnotists who use a focus for their work well know, as you stare into a crystal and enter into an alpha or meditative state, there is a tendency for many people to fall even deeper, entering a trance state. So once again, crystal gazing in particular is one method of entering trance as a trance medium, which as I explained in Chapter 3, I do not recommend.

So, how do people use scrying in their every day lives without even realizing it? Let me draw your attention to many ways you are using it yourself already. Do you remember lying on your back looking up at the clouds and then suddenly seeing a woman's face in one of them, or an animal in another? That is a beginning form of scrying. And remember waking up in the morning, and while your mind is lingering in that consciousness midway between waking and sleeping and you don't quite know you are really awake yet, you see a face peering at you from the folds of the sheets? As you become aware of what you are looking at you quickly try to focus on it, and as your mind enters a normal waking state and your focus changes, the face disappears. This is another example of beginner level scrying, and everyone does it! It happens readily when you are in that not-quite-awake stage, which is the equivalent of the alpha state we require to do most of our psychic divination work!

So, you know already that you have the ability to scry. You merely have to learn to do it consciously, and to focus your thoughts in the direction of seeing a particular thing as opposed to random objects and things.

I recall teaching a class on crystal gazing back in the 1980's in which I forgot, myself, to focus on anything specific. I saw an American army jeep traveling across the desert with a pyramid in the background and the Islamic moon and star configuration overhead. I didn't think much of it at the time, since I had asked no question and had no specific focus... until many years later, in Desert Storm and after, there were many American army jeeps there. I was being shown a political future that I failed to understand because I had no focus.

In scrying or crystal gazing it often is difficult to interpret what we see. To make this somewhat easier, I always enter my scrying meditation with a question, or a focus in mind, which I write down. I also date my page, since like many other forms of divination, my scrying may give me a look into the future. In fact, it is the nature of this form of divination to see into the future. Most of the things you see will relate to future events once you learn to scry. Nostradamas is the most famous seer in history. He used an aventurine crystal ball, combined with astrology, to scry events that would not transpire for hundreds of years. But because his focus was not specific, it is unlikely that he even understood his predictions himself at the time he wrote them down. Interpreting these images that he copiously recorded is still the work of untold numbers of scholars today.

For me, writing my focus down is imperative to both keeping my vision on target, and also to being able to interpret the things I see, so they may be of use to me and the people around me now.

Sometimes the things you see in your crystal gazing or scrying are factual. The previous image of an American army jeep in the desert is an example. This was an actual, factual representation of something to come in the future. But often the images you see are more like dream images... they are symbolic as opposed to factual. For example, I may see an image of a young man with stars floating around him. How should I interpret that, unless I have posed a question? That image could mean the young man will be a star, is moving to Texas (the star is the state symbol of Texas), is getting a promotion, or will be arrested by several sheriffs. If I have asked no question I really can't interpret this symbol at all. I can merely write it down, and wait for something to transpire that fits. If I haven't asked a question, it is possible I won't even recognize the young man. It could be a random scenario that takes place in a future not my own. But if I have posed a question, I can interpret the image relative to the question, using my experience with dream interpretation as a guide.

This is one of the reasons I have encouraged you to spend so much time on dream interpretation throughout your psychic development studies. Your dreams are a symbolic form of communication between you and your Higher Self and guides, and the better you get at interpreting them the better you will be at interpreting the psychic information received in your readings!

Types of Scrying Tools

After my description of beginning-level scrying automatically occurring when you shape clouds or do other similar activities, you will appreciate it when I tell you that you can scry in almost anything.

There used to be an old woman on Long Island everyone called the 'egg lady.' She used to take the white of an egg, put it into a clear bowl or cup with some water, give it a stir with a fork to create some ripples and depth, and scry out your future in one of the most accurate readings I've ever seen. She was wonderful at interpreting what she saw... but her use of the white of an egg in clear water was a stroke of genius. Try it when we learn the technique for crystal gazing or scrying later in the chapter. It really is very effective.

Water lends itself to scrying. As a matter of fact, water-scrying or water-divination is probably one of the easiest techniques to master. This form of divination is called a *Lunar form* (your scrying will actually be better the closer it gets to a full or new moon) and of course the moon is associated with water. I have successfully scryed in a bowl of clear water, a bowl of water with a drop of oil and a drop of vinegar swirled into it, a bowl of water with a drop of ink and a drop of oil swirled in it, water with a drop of food coloring and vinegar in it, in the bubbles of a hot tub, in a tidal pool at the beach, in a mud puddle, and in my morning coffee. I invite you to experiment with all of these once you learn the proper technique. Of course, you should never forget your protection either, unless the images you scry are totally spontaneous, which does happen sometimes. When it does, as soon as you become aware you've just received an image, write it down and date it. If you continue to scry, do your protections before you start to do it again.

So, obviously you don't have to be rich and be able to afford a real crystal ball to be able to scry. Any old puddle will do! However, many of you reading this ARE interested in purchasing or making a special scrying tool. Let me discuss some of them here with you.

Scrying mirror – These are simple thing to make. Take any concave clear glass dish and paint the outside surface flat black. You can make wormwood tea and rub the surface with the herb tea to enhance it as a scrying tool. Wormwood is an herb that enhances scrying. Or, you can purchase a fancy scrying mirror and rub it with wormwood tea. The scrying mirror you make will actually be easier to work with, because in making it you added your own vibration to it. Glass itself is an insulator, so you will find by and large that glass balls, bowls or mirrors are difficult to work with initially, until you build up enough of an energy field around them, through use, that you can readily scry in them. An experienced practitioner can easily scry in just about any surface, but a beginner does best with either a tool he or she has made, or something made of natural materials, like crystal.

Real mirror – This is not my favorite tool because it requires that you learn to focus past your own face, which many people find difficult to do. However, once the technique is mastered it is not a bad tool. Remember, though that a mirror is glass.

Acrylic crystal ball – I want to warn you against this. My own earliest crystal ball was an acrylic ball that I thought was great because it was shaped with a flat bottom, and it was huge. The first time I tried to use it I sat staring into it for three hours (not recommended) and came away with nothing more than a headache. It took many, many hours and years of use by my students in classes before that ball developed a strong enough energy field that it could lend help to the scryer.

Crystal balls – These are the most exciting. Crystal balls are made of rock crystal. These may be clear quartz, rose quartz, amethyst, or smoky quartz, all of which are mostly transparent, or of black onyx, aventurine, hematite, or other opaque stone – most people find the transparent stones easier to work with, especially ones with lots of faults and occlusions that catch the eye's fantasy. The very expensive perfectly clear quartz sphere shown in all the movies is really not as good a scrying tool as the less perfect sphere or egg or even slab of crystal that is full of cracks, bubbles, ridges, and other imperfections that catch your eye and are readily transfigured into scenes and movement as you conduct your scrying session. The real beauty of working with crystals though is that they bring their own energy to the session.

Crystal gazing, or scrying, takes enormous amounts of your energy, especially for the beginner... it helps to work with a tool that can supply some of the energy. In time, as you learn to do this you won't have to work so hard at it, and it will take much less energy to do. Until then though, it is important to keep your time that you are gazing limited, and to work with a tool that either aids your energy level, such as a crystal, or that at least does not take energy itself to use (like an acrylic ball or a glass ball).

Selecting A Crystal or Scrying Tool

A scrying implement or crystal ball is a very personal divination tool. It is NOT something that someone else should pick out for you. You should first investigate the various types of tools I've discussed, and see which ones appeal to you. Once you have narrowed it down, if the tools you are interested in are to be purchased, you should begin to shop for the exact one you want. Not all such tools are created equal, even if they look the same! The scrying tool you ultimately pick should be something that resonates to

YOU... that you feel innately comfortable with. In essence, it should be the one that jumps off the shelf and says, 'I'm it!"

I remember clearly when I first found and purchased my own crystal ball, a rather small (about 2.5 inches by 1.5 inches) smoky quartz crystal 'egg.' (Yes, you are getting the idea... when it comes to crystals size does not matter, provided the surface you are looking in is large enough for you to see an image.)

I had walked into a makeshift store that had been set up outside a seminar I was attending. From the doorway of the store I looked about 25 feet across the store to a glass display case holding crystals, and saw, from that distance, a miniature stagecoach complete with a team of four horses racing across the face of the crystal. I knew immediately it was meant to be mine, and purchased it, not even questioning a rather hefty price. I have never been sorry.

Most people don't have quite that obvious an introduction to their crystal or scrying tools. For most, it is a sense of attraction, and when you hold it, (which you should do for a while to let your own vibration merge with its) it feels right.

Charging and Caring for a Crystal or Scrying Tool

Is there anything special I should do to charge or care for my crystal or scrying tool? Yes, there is. First of all, once you have chosen your own scrying implement it will gradually become an extension of yourself, as you use it. You should not let other people touch it. Would you let someone touch intimate parts of yourself without permission? I thought not. Someone touching or using your crystal or scrying tool is really the same thing, as you will one day see.

Secondly, your scrying tool will probably need to be grounded and cleared when you first get it. Remember, many other people, from its manufacture to its sale, have undoubtedly touched it, maybe even tried it out. You will need to clear that vibration from it.

There are several ways you might go about grounding or clearing it. (Incidentally, you might also apply these to your pendulum if it should ever feel dirty to you, or if you should have trouble obtaining accurate information with it at some point.) The easiest way is to let it rest under running water for 10 or 15 minutes. In most cases this is adequate to clear a new crystal. Or, you might soak it in water with three pinches of sea salt for that same time period, or if it feels very dirty, overnight. Or try burying it or letting it rest beneath a pine, oak, or ash tree overnight. These are particularly good trees for this, since all aid the expansion of the Third Eye outward as in scrying. All will also energize your scrying tool as they ground it.

Crystal gazing or scrying is a lunar psychic ability. Your scrying implement likes the night, likes the dark, likes the moon. You should charge it by holding it in your right hand as you meditate, at night, on a full moon. When you are finished, leave it on a windowsill in the light of the full moon to finish charging. Remove it from the windowsill before sunlight. It does not like the light of the sun. It will lose its lunar charge if left in sunlight and you will have to start over again!

Your scrying implement or crystal should not be exposed to the light of day except when you are actually using it. So, you should wrap it in a soft dark natural fiber cloth like silk or cotton. Then, store it in a dark place, like a drawer or a box.

When you do your actual crystal gazing with it, you will find that you get best results in dim lighting conditions, such as in a room lit only by a candle or a dim light... you must have some light to see by, but inevitably the light will reflect in the crystal and becomes a distraction... you will need to learn to let the light that is reflected become merely one more imperfection in the ball or other tool that you are using, and that you blend into the image you will see.

You may also rub ANY scrying tool with a tea of wormwood herb or yarrow to enhance its ability to help you to scry. (Yes, that is correct. The proper tool will be a help to your scrying, not a hindrance!)

On Crystal Gazing or Scrying

Unfortunately, most of the books that I have read on crystal gazing or scrying over the years did more to confuse my natural ability to scry then they did to aid it. Most talk about the ball or scrying implement clouding over, and/or becoming hazy around the edges, and then eventually the clouds and haze disappear and you see wonderful clear images, usually around the edges of the scrying tool. This is confusing at best, and even misleading.

What clouds over is not the ball, it is your vision, as your mind shifts focus to the alpha wave level required for scrying. When you see a haze around the edges of your ball or scrying implement, it is not really that you are seeing a haze, it is that you are using the soft-focus gaze learned in Psychic Development Level 2 to see auras, which utilizes the rods, as opposed to the cones of your eyes, and produces this hazy effect around the edges.

As a reminder, you attain the alpha level by first meditating to still your mind, which is a part of our protection and invocation of guides, and you use the soft focus vision by looking obliquely, that is, indirectly, at the crystal or scrying tool – this has the affect of first clouding the edges of the crystal, then making things there appear to attain greater clarity. It forces you to look with your eyes' rod cells, the black and white receptors, as opposed to the cones, the color receptors. Any color you see in your scrying tool (and you will see color) is strictly seen clairvoyantly. Your eyes will not really see it.

And when you first see images appear out of all this, it will actually be the imperfections of the ball or implement reorganizing themselves into an image that your creative imagination is giving you. This becomes a jump off point to actually start to see images and symbols in your tool.

Now, follow the next exercise to do your first real scrying!

Exercise #1: A Technique for Crystal Gazing or Scrying

1. Darken the room and leave on only a single dim light source. Have paper and pen ready. Have your crystal ball or scrying tool set to go. Many people like to place their tool on a black cloth, finding this less distracting than the tabletop they may see through it. Sit comfortably at a table. Set an alarm clock for a 15-minute interval.

2. Be sure to turn off the phone, and be sure animals and children are where they cannot become a distraction.

3. Sit with your spine erect. Take three deep diaphragmatic breaths to ground and center. Close your eyes as you do this, and see any tension or negativity in you swirl down your body and out into the ground beneath you.

4. Place your palms in your lap facing upward, and bring as much energy as you can into yourself through them, and at the same time through your Crown Center and Third Eye Center. Breathe in as you do this, breathing in as much energy as possible. With each exhalation continue to ground.

5. When you feel clear and grounded, put yourself in the white light of protection. See Chapter 2, Exercise #3.

6. Put yourself in your protective energy balloon. Again, see Chapter 2, Exercise #3 to remember how to do this.

7. Recite your prayer. You can use your own, or the one in Chapter 2.

8. Connect with (invoke) your Protector guide and Life Guide, and your Higher Self as you learned in Chapter 2, Exercises #1 and #2. Ask for their help in your work

today. If you receive an impression that is negative, you should not proceed today, or should not ask the intended question.

9. Now, open your eyes, and date your paper and write out your question.

10. You may either pick the crystal or scrying implement up or leave it on the table and peer down into it or sideways at it. Experiment with position and placement until you find what is comfortable.

11. Gaze into the crystal. Don't stare. Your eyes should be in soft-focus. If you need to blink, go ahead. Allow your breathing to become deep and regular, and to relax your eyes still further as you breathe.

12. If your eyes want to wander around the crystal, allow them to.

13. You may or may not perceive a haze over the surface and/or around the sides of the crystal. Ignore it.

14. If you perceive an image off to the side of your gaze, do not move your eyes to look at it, just allow yourself to register the image with your peripheral vision. Continue to gaze with the same soft-focus attention and make a mental note of any other images that appear.

15. During your session, hold your mind to the best of your ability either on your question, or in a still and receptive state. If you allow it to wander, the images that appear in the crystal will either stop or become disjointed, reflecting your mental state.

16. When 15 minutes are up, bring your attention back to the room you are in, exhaling deeply to ground yourself again as you do. Write down whatever you saw, exactly as you saw it, and in sequence. Be sure to write down the seemingly inconsequential things, like a string of lights, or your own reflection that you might have seen. Once interpreted, even these things can have significance!

17. Now before you finish, thank your guides for their help, and release your protective energy balloon.

Take the time now, to interpret what you saw in light of the question you had asked.

Congratulations! You have just completed your first controlled scrying session. In time you can become very adept at this, and it may even become one of your tools of choice for obtaining future information.

You should also note that practice with scrying will be an invaluable aid to developing your clairvoyant skills to where you can begin to see people and symbols around other people, in their energy fields. And eventually, if you decide to study spirit communication (mediumship) it will help you to develop the ability to see the spirits clairvoyantly as well.

End of Chapter Exercises

1. Continue to record your dreams.

2. Continue to record your psychic experiences.

3. Continue to meditate.

4. Continue to do your Chakra Meditation daily.

5. Send and receive a telepathic message with a partner – in this exercise send a scene with a person in it, and a one-word message. Don't forget to do your remote viewing.

6. Continue to practice your psychometry, your pendulum work, and your automatic writing.

7. Obtain a scrying crystal, crystal ball, or scrying tool of your choice, and practice with it for at least 15 minutes a day.

8. Try a group healing. Have a friend choose someone he or she would like to send healing energy to. Mentally visualize the person and ask him if it's okay to send healing. If he says yes, proceed. This one friend will focus the energy and send it to the ill person since he or she knows him. He will also receive the healing energy sent by the other participants, and send it on. Get a group of additional friends together. If this is to be done in person sit in a circle. If participants are distant from one another have them use the energy screen to focus energy to the person acting as the focus. Have them all go into a guided visualization to their own workplaces. Have them focus three rays of energy, one from the heart, one from the Third Eye, and one from the crown to the friend who is focusing the energy. That friend in turn will focus those same three rays of energy on the Higher Self of the friend being healed. Hold the focus and continue to send energy for about three minutes then release each ray of energy. Get feedback!

Suggested Reading

- *Crystal Balls & Crystal Bowls* by Andrews
- *Scrying for Beginners* by Tyson
- *Crystal Gazing* (Cassette) by Sandy Anastasi

Chapter 6

Other Popular Forms of Divination

There are many other popular forms of divination and psychic reading that are beyond the scope of this book to discuss or instruct in, since they are themselves in-depth courses of study. In fact, some are considered lifelong disciplines. Let's discuss some of these so that you have a passing familiarity with them, and also so that you know enough about them that you may wish to take up a separate study of them.

Tarot Cards and Standard Deck Card Reading

Card reading is one of the oldest forms of divination, and is certainly the most popular form of divination utilized by most psychics today, as an alternative, or in addition to straight psychic readings. It is also an easy and quick form of divination to learn the basics of. Essentially, all you need do is learn the meanings of the cards, which are usually based on universal symbolism, and how to interpret those meanings within the context of a card layout. Learning to read the cards is a matter of several months; however, becoming good at them can be the work of several years of constant practice. It is easier to learn Tarot cards that are fully illustrated than a standard playing card deck that is not.

Tarot card reading has several advantages for the psychic. As you slowly learn the meanings of the cards you develop a sort of automatic protection that forms around you as you lay the cards out, and is absorbed back into you as you pick them up at the end of your reading. The cards also supply an intermediary between you and the client, much like the pendulum does, so it is easier to remain apart from the client's vibration than it is in straight type readings. Also, since the cards are not dependent upon psychic energy (they really do tell the story all by themselves – your psychic insight is helpful, but not necessary) if a client is blocking you from doing a straight psychic reading you can just read the cards. Usually when this happens the accuracy of the cards gets him (or her) to drop his wall so that you can reach through to do your regular psychic reading.

And one of the best things about the Tarot cards is that they do train your mind to be psychically receptive, over time, and they do it in a safe way.

I highly recommend the study of the Tarot for anyone who is tool oriented, and who would like a truly excellent one to fall back on when your psychic readings need that extra boost.

I have published another book, *The Tarot Reader's Workbook* on the subject. I also have a complete line of audiotapes and CD's available for Tarot students on my Web site, www.SandyAnastasi.com.

Runes

Rune divination, like Tarot card reading, is a very old form of divination that originated in the Scandinavian area. It is actually simpler to learn than Tarot reading, since there are less symbols to learn, but is much more intuitive so it takes longer to become really skilled. Runes are Viking symbols, or letters, usually carved on stones. However, today you see runes drawn or carved on wood, plastic, metal, bone, pottery, and just about any other medium you can imagine. When runes are carved into crystal they are especially powerful to work with since, as when in the last chapter you worked with an actual crystal for divination, the crystal supplies additional energy for the reading. Many people who work with runes also see them as a magical language that carries its own very special intrinsic energy with it.

Ouija Boards

These represent a form of divination I try to dissuade people from bothering with. First of all, for an experienced psychic who has learned the many techniques for divination previously discussed in this book, the Ouija board is far too slow to be worth using. Your automatic writing is faster and more effective. Secondly, for someone inexperienced yet psychically gifted and unprotected, they can be devastating. Those of you who are interested in horror stories about possession should rent the old movie *Witch Board*. This movie has special affects that are a little far out, but the story line is an accurate description of how someone can become possessed through using a Ouija board without protection, if the person is psychically open. It is very similar to the story I told earlier about my student who had attracted a negative entity through automatic writing without protection.

But if you simply MUST play with a Ouija board, please do it with the full protection you learned in Chapter 2 and have been using throughout this book.

I remember many years ago, working a Ouija board with a friend's daughter. The girl had a bad experience with Angel Dust (an illegal recreational drug of the 70's) and had started talking to a lot of entities that only she could see. She was also behaving very strangely... her mother wanted to communicate with them through a Ouija board, to see if they were really there, and if they were as harmful as she thought they were. Her mother brought her to me so that she could do it safely. I protected us, and we began to use the board. I was amazed that as each entity came through the energy entirely changed. All were unpleasant. All were the low-level spirits, human and non-human, that usually do come through when a Ouija board is employed. As each came through, I recognized the energy as unhealthy, and sent it away. This freed the girl temporarily from the influence of these entities, but unless she received professional psychiatric care, she only invited them back later out of loneliness.

On another occasion, I had a different friend actually become possessed herself when using a Ouija board. Unfortunately, it was my board that I had loaned her, so in this instance I felt somewhat to blame when she began coming in to work every morning exhausted because she'd stayed up all night working the board alone. Back then I didn't even believe in Ouija boards so I found it hard to believe that a grown woman was playing this foolish game alone... what I mean is, I thought it was foolish until the day I actually saw something not human looking out of her eyes at me. I went straight to her house, repossessed the board I had lent her, and took it home to work with it myself to see if she could REALLY be doing that with it. As soon as I touched it, the plastic pointer began to move by itself. She had definitely drawn something to the board... I found after a few minutes that I could not readily remove my fingers from the plastic pointer – they were stuck to it as if a low grade electrical current was passing through it. I finally managed to remove my fingers from the board and proceeded to burn it. Next, I rounded up my girlfriend and took her to an exorcist.

I hope I have made my point. For the educated, Ouija boards are a waste of time; there are much more accurate, direct, and satisfying methods of communicating with your Higher Self, guides, and departed loved ones. For the gifted amateur they are a great danger. I do wish that Toys 'R' Us would stop carrying them!

Palmistry

Palmistry is another very old divination tool. It is the art of reading and interpreting the various lines and markings on your hands. It is most often used for character analysis (and quite accurately) today, but can also be used as a predictive tool by experienced practitioners. It is very easy to learn the basics of Palmistry, but if you choose to become a REAL palmist, expect years of study and practice ahead of you. I worded that 'become a REAL palmist' because most palmists that I have met (some of them even very good palmists who taught palmistry) stop being palmists and become psychometrists as soon as they take their clients hand in their own. If you see a palmist looking at your face or at the ceiling or off into space when he (or she) is reading your palm, rest assured he is NOT reading the lines on your hand! More likely, he is reading your vibration – which may even give you a better reading, but is no longer Palmistry! I do not consider myself a good palmist – but I have studied the art of Palmistry for many years, and would definitely encourage anyone to learn it. As an adjunct to your straight psychic readings it is an excellent tool. Also, it has been used as a divination tool for so many centuries, that you will find that many clients automatically ask for it.

Tea Leaf or Coffee Ground Reading

The art of Tea Leaf Reading or Coffee Ground Reading in its original form is actually another form of scrying. Your practice with the exercises in Chapter 4 will certainly help you to be able to do this well. Usually the tea or coffee is drunk as close to the bottom of the cup as possible, and then the cup is turned over to eliminate any remaining liquid. Finally it is righted again, and the placement of the leaves or grounds in the cup is what gives you your reading. When you read tea leaves using a scrying technique, be sure to remember to protect yourself as we learned in Chapter 2. But there are many ways of reading tea leaves or coffee grounds, and not all involve scrying. There are astrological methods, and all kinds of other methods that employ various circular patterns and layouts that tell you information based upon where the leaves or grounds fall in the cup, after the tea or coffee has been drunk.

Graphology

Graphology is the art of handwriting analysis, which has become accepted in the scientific and legal communities as accurate enough to use in a courtroom, not only for identification purposes, but also for personality analysis. I once worked with a friend who was studying Graphology at a college in New York City; he had an assignment to analyze a doodle, using the graphs and tools his instructor had supplied him with. He brought his results to me, and asked me to psychometrize the doodle as well (note that it was a photocopy, yet I could still use it to link in through psychometry). When we were both finished with our mutual personality analysis of the doodle, he concluded, "Wow, this sounds like Charles Manson. Bet it's him!" Well, when he went to class the next day it was the instructor who was surprised – it was indeed a doodle done by Charles Manson during his trial. And we were able to draw that conclusion through using the combination of Graphology and Psychometry. Astonishing.

Numerology

Numerology is the art of reading numbers as symbols. Each number has a different meaning, symbolically, and how they are put together affects how they affect you. You have numbers all around you. There is your street address, your birthday, and even the letters in your name can easily be converted to numbers (A=1, B=2, C=3, and so on through the alphabet). Your numbers can tell a numerologist about your personality, your relationships, your childhood, your life's challenges, and even things about your future. The basics of Numerology can be learned quickly and easily, yet to become truly adept at it can take many years of study.

Astrology

Astrology is the oldest science in the world. It is said that all other sciences arose out of astrology. Astrology is the study of how the planets affect our lives. It is based upon the study of a birth chart that plots the positions of the planets at the time and place of your birth, and then evaluates the affects of where those same planets are right now, on the natal positions. Astrology can be used for amazingly accurate character profiling, and is also an awesome divination tool when used for prediction. Most astrologers treat astrology as a science, not as a psychic divination tool, yet I know many psychics who use astrology as a jumping off point for their psychic readings. The basics of Astrology can be learned quickly, but to become good at this requires years of study. Those people reading this who are interested in the study of Astrology might begin their studies with my book, *Astrology: Art and Science*.

There are also many other forms of divination – Iridology, is the art of reading the iris of the eye. There is a divination science for reading the bumps on your head (seriously!), a technique of throwing bones or shells, and many other systems that have evolved in various cultures all over the planet. These are just the major ones. All can be used as an adjunct to straight psychic readings, all help you to open and develop your intuition in a controlled and mostly safe manner (with the exception of the Ouija board as noted previously, that is!).

End of Chapter Exercises

1. Continue to practice all of the exercises listed at the end of Chapter 4.

2. Continue to meditate daily and to do your Chakra Exercise Daily.

3. Continue to record your psychic experiences.

4. With a friend, do this telepathy exercise – send and receive a scene, with both a feeling or emotion, and a word attached to it. Remember to do your remote viewing.

5. Select one or more divination tools from this chapter and research them further. On the following page is an extensive list of suggested reading available to support each area. Decide which, if any, you would like to add to your psychic repertoire.

Suggested Reading

On Tarot

- *Astrology: Art and Science* by Sandy Anastasi
- *Easy Tarot Guide* by Martin

On Astrology

- *Beginner's Astrology Workbook* by Sandy Anastasi
- *Alan Oken's Complete Astrology* by Alan Oken
- *The Astrologer's Handbook* by Sakioan and Acker

On Palmistry

- *The Complete Book of Palmistry* by Webster
- *Instant Palm Reader: A Roadmap to Life* by Domin

On Graphology

- *Graphology for Beginners* by Craze
- *Elements of Graphology* by Branston

Coffee & Tea Leaf Reading

- *Fortune in a Coffee Cup: Divination with Coffee Grounds* by Sophia
- *Tea Leaf Reading* by Hewitt

Ouija

- *Ouija: The Most Dangerous Game* by Hurt

Automatic Writing

- *Automatic Writing & Heroscripting* by Stockwell
- *Automatic Writing* (cassette) by Sandy Anastasi

Chapter 7

The Art of Astral Traveling

Astral Travel is Natural to Everyone

Astral traveling is totally natural. We all do it already. It is part of the natural sleep process that we experience every night. I am sure you have experienced that sensation, when you are just drifting off into sleep and suddenly wake up feeling like you were falling? The sensation of falling may have been so real that when you woke you were surprised momentarily to find the solid bed beneath you. Actually, you were really not falling at all. As you were drifting into sleep your astral body had already begun to separate from your physical body, when something brought you back to waking consciousness and caused your astral body to snap back into the physical. You weren't falling at all; the sensation of falling was your consciousness moving from the astral body back into the physical so quickly. That alone should prove to you that you really are astral traveling every night!

All of us do this; it is perfectly natural. This makes it sound like astral traveling on purpose, that is, consciously, should be easy, doesn't it? It is not.

Most people experience waking out-of-body experiences only rarely, and usually under traumatic circumstances. For example, a sudden burst of pain can cause you to suddenly jump from you body to escape the pain. That is also a normal human response. The result usually leaves you suspended above yourself looking down for a moment or two, before you snap back in. Of course, while you are out there looking down, the rest of the world thinks your physical body, which has suddenly gone limp, has fainted. Extreme emotional trauma can initiate a similar response. But these types of experiences are rare, and also lack conscious control.

Since we are usually asleep when we are astral traveling, and most of us are not conscious while we are asleep, at best we have odd memories of being out of the body. We may remember flying in our dreams, or remember dreams in vivid, intense colors, or dreams that were so real we thought we were awake... but most of us would be surprised, to say the least, to find out that in those dreams we had left our physical bodies behind, in bed, while our astral body took on a life of its own on the other planes.

And yet it is both normal and natural for us to do just that. Scientists know that we dream nightly; in fact, they know that we must dream to stay alive, although they don't know why. Studies have shown that when allowed to sleep, but wakened just before dream-sleep sets in, people begin to first become irritable, then begin to lose mental clarity, then gross motor skills, and finally fine motor skills and the autonomic muscle and nervous impulses that keep our body running (i.e., if we don't dream when we sleep, we ultimately die). I believe it is not the dream-sleep that we need, but the out-of-body experiences that occur for most people ONLY during dream sleep that we need to stay alive. In fact, I believe that we do an energy recharge while in the astral body each night that can occur in no other way. It is without this recharge that we die.

As we develop our psychic abilities, we gain an extraordinary ability for mental focus, combined with an ability to relax our physical body totally, and an ability to move in and out of what we call the alpha brain wave state to do our psychic work. All of this leads to more intense dreaming, better dream recall, and ultimately an ability to wake up in our dreams, called *lucid dreaming*.

Lucid Dreaming Helps to Learn Astral Traveling

Lucid dreaming is very good practice for astral travel. There is an exercise later in this chapter that will help your ability to lucid dream, and through that, lead to an improved ability for astral travel.

It is when we become aware in our dreams that we are dreaming that we begin to recognize some of our dreams are more real than others. Some are in brighter, almost incandescent colors. In some, we actually seem to have real control of events. And in some, we visit places in our dreams, and interact with them, and then we revisit them during our waking life a day or two later. We begin to realize that we have, in truth, really been there – just not in our physical form.

As you read the words above, you realized that you have had many dreams such as these; you have astral traveled. We have ALL astral traveled in our dreams.

But to bring this natural ability for astral travel through dreams to a conscious tool that the waking mind can use is no small feat.

To Astral Travel Consciously is One Goal of Adepts and Mystics

To astral travel consciously is one of the goals of adepts in almost every magical and mystical tradition in the world. The reasons for this are multiple. First, as the Aboriginal culture in Australia believes, the dream world is the real world and this physical world is the dream. Another way of saying this is that the dream world we can enter deliberately through conscious astral travel and which give us access to both the lower and upper astral planes is the causative plane to this one. (See Chapter 3, Figure 4, for my schematic on the planes.)

Changes that we make on these higher levels are swiftly reflected down here on the physical plane.

Here is a simple example; if I have an argument with my friend, who is being bullheaded and simply not listening to what I am saying, I can visit her on the astral plane during sleep (or even consciously during the day, if I have learned to utilize this ability while I am awake) and continue my discussion with her on a higher level, where she will be more inclined to listen. In this way, we can readily resolve our differences so that the next time I encounter her on the physical level we will be understanding one another instead of arguing over unimportant issues. Mind you, I am very careful not to use coercion on her while she is in her receptive dream sleep. That is actually black magic – it is ALWAYS wrong to impose your will on another person, even if you feel you are right! The backlash to you is incredible, by the way – since like attracts like, it invites someone else to impose his or her will on you in an equally sneaky way!

Astral travel can do much more than that, too. You can consciously visit places that are at a great distance from you. This includes distant places geographically, as well as past lives, and other planes of existence. My own first experience talking with someone who had died was when I astral traveled onto the other planes and visited my grandmother after her death.

You can visit people and give them subliminal messages as well; if they are in a receptive frame of mind, they will receive those messages. One student I had in a former class practiced his astral traveling at the gym he frequented. He had arrived late, and on his way in asked the person at the snack bar to have a hamburger and a coke ready for him when he was done. After his workout, while in the sauna, he decided to practice his astral traveling. He employed the exercise at the end of this chapter to get himself into it, then left his body, floated out to the snack bar, looked the counterman in the eye and said, "Change that to a bagel and orange juice, will you?" Well, when he came out the bagel and juice were waiting for him. The counterman, when asked, knew he had changed his order, but couldn't precisely remember when. He just knew my student had told him to. You will need to experiment yourself in much the same way, once you have learned how to do this, because it is only this direct kind of proof that will really convince you that you are doing it, since your physical body doesn't go anywhere!

There are many magical traditions around the planet where the Shaman performing a rite will go into trance to accomplish the intended goal. That trance is actually a self-induced deep sleep for the body that frees the astral body to go out on the astral plane and accomplish the work, which might include anything from getting crops to grow more swiftly to putting a protective wall around their home or village or performing a healing on someone.

Followers of Sai Baba, a well known mystic and Indian sage, report seeing him and talking with him thousands of miles from his home in India, which he never left. Some even claim to have seen him in different places at the same time.

Thought travels far faster than the speed of light, and astral travel, which occurs on the airy and mental astral planes, involves moving at the speed of thought. It is entirely possible that Sai Baba could have been seen at essentially the same time by followers in different places.

Relaxation: a Pre-Requisite to Astral Traveling

The first step to being able to astral travel is being able to totally relax. This is why most people only astral during sleep. For the etheric or astral body to separate from the physical requires that you thoroughly relax the physical, or there is too much tension between the physical and astral for the astral body to separate.

Since you have learned how to totally relax your body while keeping your mind crisp and clear, you have already learned the first steps in astral travel. Our exercise to astral travel at the end of the chapter begins with a complete 10-point relaxation.

Protection of the Physical Body During Astral Traveling

Shamans that use astral travel as part of their magical practice understand an important thing about the process. While the astral body is out of the physical body, the physical body needs to be held safe. Usually a Shaman engaged in astral travel will have a person keep watch over the body until he returns to it. For most people who astral travel only at night while they sleep this is not an issue, since the worst that might happen is your arm going to sleep, which only causes you to return to the body to relieve the discomfort and then leave again. You do this so smoothly that it is not an issue at all. But when you are astral traveling while awake, more precautions need to be taken since the circumstances around your physical body can change swiftly. You don't want to do your astral traveling while driving, or in a public place, or when you are in any physically precarious position, for example.

Many people fear to astral travel because they are afraid that they will not be able to get back into their physical body again, once they are out of it. Rest assured, you do this every night and you have not failed to get back into yourself yet. When out of body, all you need do, really, is think about being back in your physical body and almost immediately you will be. I have a good friend who is a great astral traveler, and she reports an early experience of having a great time floating around her bedroom and watching herself sleep until she realized she didn't know how to get back into her body. She tried diving in, climbing in, laying on top of herself, nothing worked! Finally, in a state of panic, she let go of trying and just relaxed – instantly she was back in. Her fear was a mental focus that actually kept her from getting back in. When on the astral, you travel with the power of your mind. That is important to remember. I will discuss that at greater length later.

Many clairvoyants report seeing what is now commonly referred to as the *silver cord* extending between the astral form and the physical body when someone is out of the body. This silver cord links the two bodies together and allows for the transference of life-force energy and consciousness between the two bodies when you are out of body. It is this cord that gives you the sensation of falling when you suddenly snap back into the body too quickly. Shaman and frequent astral travelers are aware that as long as this cord is intact it will always pull the astral body back to the physical when the astral journey is done. However, if it is severed, the physical body dies. This is what happens at death. It is also the chief reason why Shamans with enemies are always sure to have someone they trust keep watch while they are out. They often call astral traveling *dream walking*.

The amount of life-force energy that travels down the silver cord from the physical body into the astral body is important, too, because it determines the level or depth of the astral experience.

Levels of Astral Travel

There are two main types of astral travel, one of which you have been doing a variation of when you do your remote viewing. That is mind travel. Most of you, when you do your remote viewing, focus on a target and view it and the surroundings. But I am sure some of you have become engrossed enough to really focus on the subject of your remote viewing, to the point of actually feeling like you had moved into the room with the person you were viewing. This feeling of having traveled in your mind is real, and it is the first level of real astral travel. This is a form of mind travel. On a mental level, you sent enough energy down the link to this subject, that a part of your consciousness actually visited them.

In mind travel though, even though you definitely feel that you are there, other than telepathy you can have no affect on your subject or your environment.

The next level is actual astral travel. This level is achieved after you have established the mind travel link as you continue to put more of your life-force energy through the link and through your sliver cord to the part of you that is with the subject. Usually, this is done through physical interaction with the subject and his environment. You use that interaction to draw more of your life-force energy into the mental astral image you are seeing, until you are feeling so strongly there that in a limited way (as noted above) you can interact with the environment.

So, you see, your remote viewing expands into mind travel that expands into astral travel. And it doesn't stop there.

Astral travel itself has many levels of involvement with the target. It all depends on how much of your life-force energy from your physical body is drawn through the link to the astral body. The lowest level of astral travel would involve putting just enough energy through the link to be able to feel and sense the material environment around the subject. At the extreme other end would be putting enough through to become visible to the target subject. Or perhaps to even interact with the physical plane. I do believe, for example, that if enough life force could be put through that link it would be perfectly possible to pick up and transport an object back with you when you return to your body. However, for most of us it would be dangerous to pour enough of our own life force through that link to, for example, become physically visible to the target we are visiting. Yet for someone like Sai Baba, who has developed an energy far beyond most people on the planet right now, visibly appearing will not draw so much of him through the link as to kill him. Usually, if you see someone who is astraling in this manner, it is because he (or she) has emitted a quick burst of emotion over something that makes him momentarily visible, and also, the people who see him are usually in an altered state themselves, for example, if they had been daydreaming they'd be in an alpha state receptive to seeing or hearing something on the astral. But someone like Sai Baba could become visible to a subject that was in a normal mindset and was otherwise occupied; this entails far more life force than the rest of us could muster, let alone put through the link.

Yes, there are people in our world today who have reached that stage of evolution, and it should be a stimulus to the rest of us to seek to develop ourselves.

There are also various planes and sub-planes that our astral travel will take place upon.

Astral Planes and Sub-Planes

A friend who was a bit afraid of astral travel, but who had done it numerous times with conscious awareness asked me once, "Sandy, what are those 'little people' I see crawling all over my body whenever I come in and out of it?"

Most of us don't see this, but in fact, the lowest plane of the astral, lying just above the physical that is called the etheric plane, and upon which our etheric aura actually lies, is filled with these little elemental creatures that some people can see on the astral, others don't see at all, and still others just see as flecks of light. All of us move through this plane, and through them, every time we enter or exit the body in astral travel, which is to say, every night. We usually do this so quickly they don't even register on us, unless we decide to hang around, as my friend did, to watch them. They are harmless. They are also not the only things you will encounter on this lowest of the astral planes. This is the plane of thoughtforms, and we humans create them with great alacrity. You are liable to encounter anything from someone's nightmare of Godzilla here to the sexiest lady in the latest *Playboy* magazine. Nothing on this level can hurt you, unless you buy into it. Remember, some of those thoughtforms you encounter may involve addictions, or low-level entities looking for a place to get energy – you. Most of us will have no problem on this level because we pass through it so quickly we hardly notice it. But people who have negative attitudes, or are involved with a low element in their waking lives, could more readily remain on this level, in which case astral travel for them would seem much like a horror movie.

But most of us will immediately pass through this etheric astral plane without even noticing it. And above it we find the sub-levels of the lower and upper astral planes. The lower astral planes (again, let me refer you back to Chapter 3, Figure 4) are where we will travel to other parts of this planet, visit things and people that are a part of our physical and material reality. The upper part of the lower astral, and the upper astral, are far separated from the physical plane. Upon them we can visit with deceased relatives as I did, or go to school, or meet with your guides, or even encounter and interact with fellow astral travelers. In fact, we do just that every night.

How to Move on the Astral

Moving through the astral planes is totally natural in the dream state, so you would think that when people learned to astral travel consciously the ability to move naturally there would just follow right through. Unfortunately, it doesn't. So, I'll give you some basic rules to follow, and you will just have to use them as guidelines until you develop experience yourself.

The first and most important basic rule is that since the entire astral plane is literally formed of the stuff of mind, the only way to move around and navigate through it is with your mind.

And, of course, that sounds easy, until the first time you are experimenting with astraling to visit your mother and as you are just leaving your body a passing thought about eating pancakes crosses your mind and you find yourself instantly in the local pancake house.

So you can see, astral traveling successfully requires very good mind control.

It is important not only to have decided ahead of time where you want to visit... it is also important to maintain your focus as you travel. The slightest passing thought will take you instantly to the new location!

Also, since movement occurs on the astral via thought, not feet, it is very interesting to watch newcomers who try to walk or run. It doesn't work at all. The only way you can walk or run on the astral is if you think of yourself walking or running. The same thing is true of flying, though flying is a good way to navigate the astral because even though our mind must still move us, the concept of flying allows us to move swiftly, yet stay in touch with what we are looking at as we pass over it.

And remember the idea of the planes. If you should ever encounter anything disturbing to you while astral traveling, you need only think up to the next plane, and any negative or low-level thing that you have encountered will be left behind as you move to a higher level of the astral. Also, as you learn to navigate, know that moving sideways on the same level keeps you in the same plane, whereas going up and down moves through the planes. Eventually, as you become good at this, you may even be gifted with the ability to clairvoyantly see that *psychic web* I have spoken about all through this series, the web that links all things together, even through they may exist on different levels.

Identifying Things on the Astral

Things on the astral look different. Because the astral plane is a plane of mental energy, material things tend to take on symbolic appearance there, as well as actual appearance.

For example, you might see your friend on the astral as looking like something she is doing or involved with, rather than like herself. If she is acting very childish you will probably see her as a child. If she is at a happy time in her life, and she has associated a happy time in the past with a rose garden, you might see her in a rose garden. If she is dating a man who is a con artist you might see Paul Newman in his role in *The Sting* instead of her actual boyfriend.

Or you might see an old friend that you haven't been in touch with for a long while, but who was going through something similar to what this current friend is. Perhaps the old friend and the current one keep interchanging positions on the astral when you see them. You see one face imposed over the other.

Or perhaps you are visiting a friend's house, but the furniture is arranged opposite to what it really is. This phenomenon is extremely common when viewing things on the astral.

Or perhaps you recognize elements of two or even three houses that you are visiting all put together. This is because you do see the material plane reflected upward into the astral, but the mind-stuff of that plane is giving you other information as well. Perhaps the person you are visiting is living in one of those houses, but has stuff going on in his or her life that reflects similar issues in both of those other houses.

I clearly recall astraling to visit an old boyfriend's family home and mother (mothers have always made me nervous) before I met her. I 'flew' down a straight road, came to a winding curve to the right that was tree-lined, and then flew up to the front door of the house, passing a garage on my left along the way. The door opened and a tiny woman with swift bird-like movements met me.

When I actually saw this place later on with my physical eyes, I was surprised. The road passing the house was straight. The winding tree lined curve to the right was not a part of the road as I had seen, but a curving drive leading up to the door. The garage on the left was not a garage, but a small guest house. From the ground the property looked entirely different than it had from the air. This is also very common when astral traveling. Things look different because your perspective is different.

Incidentally, my description of his mother was perfectly accurate, even to the bird-like movements. But on the astral they were exaggerated so that you could readily see they were a character trait. Likewise, it is not uncommon to see someone with a big mouth on the astral, indicating they talk a lot, or can't keep a secret.

On the astral plane color is also experienced very vividly, so don't expect to visit a place later on and see the same intensity of color.

One other astral experience I had when teaching adult education is worth describing here, too, if only for its humor. I was scheduled to teach a class in a school I was not familiar with, so I scouted ahead a day or so ahead of time to get the lay of the land, so to speak. When I looked at the classroom I was to be in, I saw it filled with unruly children throwing things, talking out of turn, and just being generally annoying. I assumed what I saw was the class that was occupying the room when I astraled into it to peak. I was wrong. The day I taught the class, the adults in those seats behaved exactly as those children had…. when I really looked at them, I actually recognized some of the children I had seen. I had apparently astraled into the future to my actual class without realizing it. I saw the adults as children because that is exactly how they behaved.

Methods of Getting Out of the Body

Over the years I have tried as many methods for leaving the body during astral travel as I have read books on the subject, and that is a considerable amount.

I astral traveled in dreams consciously for as long as I can remember. Yet being able to leave the body at will while I was awake eluded me. I was only finally able to do that when I started using the technique I will show you a bit later, in Exercise #1. I have since found that most of my students achieve good results with this as well.

However, I must put forward a disclaimer at this point… just about everything else I teach (except perhaps seeing the colors in the aura) I know just about every student will accomplish. Astral traveling is different. It really is something you have to do on your own. All I can do here is to tell you as many techniques as I've learned, emphasize the one that most of my students achieve the most success with, and encourage you to go practice!

I have experimented with all of these techniques with varying degrees of success. However, all of them require that your body be completely relaxed first. As a matter of fact, most people who fail to achieve success with astral traveling will fail because they did not take the time to get their physical bodies out of the way by putting them to sleep. If you have not yet mastered the 10-point relaxation exercise presented in every book of this series, I suggest you go back now and do so. By now you need to be good enough at it that you can relax a part of your body merely by thinking about it and the number associated with it in the relaxation, and saying to yourself, 'Relax, sleep.' (You will forever be grateful to me because this will prevent you from ever again getting a charlie horse that you can't quickly get rid of!)

1. The first technique I ever experimented with entailed doing a complete relaxation, and when your body was totally relaxed, you rolled sideways out of it and onto the astral. I unfortunately landed on the floor. I wish you better luck.

2. The second technique was similar to the first one, only instead of rolling out sideways you do a sort of backward roll out of your head. Likewise, whenever I

tried to do this my physical body came along for the ride, seemingly no matter how relaxed I was. I have since learned that I can achieve success with both of these techniques if after fully relaxing my body I visualize myself rolling out, as opposed to actually doing it.

3. A third technique involves visualizing your life-force energy that animates your physical body flowing into a spinning ball at your Crown Center, your Solar Plexus Center, your Heart Center, or your Sacral Center and then breathing it out that center. You become an energy being shaped like you floating in the air above the center. With practice you project your consciousness out of the chosen center along with the life-force energy. I have had more success with this technique than the other two, but all three of these techniques are really for advanced travelers; beginners are bound to find difficulty with them.

4. There is also a simple technique of sitting up in a chair, doing your 10-point relaxation, allowing separation to occur, and then just standing up out of your physical body. Again, this is easy for regular travelers to accomplish, but difficult for beginners.

5. A fifth technique of astral traveling is a bit more difficult to orchestrate, but considerably more effective than these. After fully relaxing your physical body, visualize a complete you standing next to you (you are lying down, eyes are closed). Once you have completed the visualization, transfer your consciousness to the energy you standing next to you. As you succeed in looking at your prone body through eyes that are looking down at it you will realize that you have successfully left your body and are firmly in the astral you. The only drawback I have found to this technique is that for a beginner, it challenges reality. Many people begin to achieve success here, only to lose it when they find themselves looking down at their own body. Having been trained from childhood that this is not possible, for many looking down at your own body causes a snap-back of the consciousness into the body. This technique, like the above ones, is therefore more often successful to the advanced traveler.

The physical body tends to hold on to the astral form while you are awake. That occurs as a result of our unconscious need to hold on to life (but that is not the subject of this book). That is one reason why you must be fully relaxed physically for separation of the two to occur. Am I saying that if you are comfortable with the idea of death it is easier to astral travel? Why yes, I guess I am! Perhaps that also is one reason why, for many, learning to astral travel alleviates the fear of death. We discover when we astral that we are, in fact, more than our physical body! It is truly a wonderful experience!

But for many, even complete relaxation is not enough for the astral body to break free of the physical. For people who are good at feeling sensations the experience of speed and spinning can be just the thing to snap the astral body free. In Exercise #1 we will be employing this along with another technique, but if you want, try it alone. For many people, focusing on speed and spinning your consciousness out of one of your chakras as above, or just focusing intently on the sensations is enough to cause separation to occur. If you have ever fainted, you will recall that dizziness that you are still experiencing when you wake up? Now you know why you have it!

6. The technique I find most effective for beginners and experienced travelers alike is simple. Form follows thought. One of the most effective means for leaving the body that I have found to date is to use your thought to cause the astral body to project. First, relax the physical body with your 10-point relaxation, then use remote viewing to focus on a target. Then, while remaining focused, use the technique of employing speed and spinning to travel down the link to the target. I visualize a hallway or tunnel linking me to my target to make the link more tangible to me. Next, to anchor in to the target, you focus on as many physical sensations around it as you can. You feel the surfaces of objects, smell scents in the air, and interact with the target and its location as much as possible to settle your consciousness into your astral form that is now at the target location. The more completely you make the sensation connections, the more complete will be your transfer of consciousness from the physical body the astral body. Exercise #1 will demonstrate this technique, and several others that become simple to use once you have experienced 'getting out' for the first time!

7. Another very effective aid to learning to astral travel is to incorporate Hemi-Sync tapes into your exercises. The Monroe Institute of Applied Sciences in Fabor, Virginia, has created a complete line of such tapes. They use sound to alter your brain waves in such a way as to induce an astral experience in many people. The Hemi-Sync technology puts a single tone into one ear and a different tone into the other; your brain hears the difference. This forces both brain hemispheres to become perfectly synchronized, which produces the brain pattern required for astral traveling.

8. Of course, for anyone, learning to become conscious in your astral dreams is the best way to become comfortable with the process of astral travel. Once you are comfortable with it in the dream state, it is much easier to accomplish while waking. To help you to develop lucid dreaming I've included an exercise below, originally published in *Omni Magazine* many years back. If you work on this for two weeks before beginning your practice with these astral travel techniques, or even while you are practicing them, you will achieve better results more swiftly.

'Omni' Dream Experiment

Step 1: To Start Lucid Dreaming

To facilitate lucid dreaming, you should ask yourself often during the course of the day whether you are dreaming. Each time you ask this question look for evidence that shows you are NOT dreaming. For example, read something, look away and then look back and read it again. If it is the same when you look back, you are not dreaming. After you have proved in this manner that you are NOT dreaming, visualize yourself doing something you would like to do. Tell yourself right after that you want to recognize a dream at night the next time it occurs – coupling these things together will help you to remember the next time you dream, while you are dreaming. If you wake up from a dream, go back to it immediately in your imagination; if your intention is strong and clear enough you might find yourself awake in your dreams as you return to sleep.

Step 2: Dream Flying

Dream flying is important, because according to noted psychologists LaBerge and Gackenbach, developers of this exercise, it is a form of dream control that is easy to do. It gives you a sense of freedom and it is a basic means of travel in dreams. I also would add, that it trains you to astral travel in the dream state. So, while you are conducting this experiment on yourself, concentrate on dream flight. In your dreams if you are falling, turn the fall into flying. If you are merely traveling, don't walk, run, or drive... fly. But how do you get yourself to fly in your dreams? Before going to bed each night, rub your Third Eye as we do to remember our dreams, but say, "Tonight, I will fly in my dreams." Then, take a moment to imagine your dream flight, to pre-program your unconscious mind. Then later, if you find yourself flying, and say, "This is a dream." As you begin to be able to wake to flying in a dream, gradually take control and experiment with different types of flying (i.e., floating, increasing altitude and speed, and maneuvering). Ask yourself questions such as "How high can I fly, or can I travel so fast that I experience the sensation of pure speed?" Asking the question will help you to attain the experience. The last question, about speed, is most important, because it is one of the methods used to leave the body to enter the astral plane, as I noted above.

Step 3: Dream Spinning

Even lucid dreamers often wake up in mid-dream. It is hard to get your mind to stay asleep once it realizes it is dreaming. Also, when you try to take control of a dream, it often creates enough of a normal waking awareness state that it wakes you up. The idea is to stay asleep, be awake in the dream, and take control of it so that you are making it happen the way you want it to. LaBerge and Gackenback found, in their years of dream research, and that spinning your dream body can sustain the period of sleep, prevent you from waking, and give you greater dream control. I find this interesting because my own experience in astral traveling has shown me that spinning the dream or astral body is another way of moving onto the astral plane. To practice dream spinning, you start before you go to bed, just like you did with dream flying. Before going to bed, decide on a person, a time, and a place you would like to visit in your dream. This person and place can be real, imaginary, past, present, or future. Write down your target, memorize it, and then visualize yourself visiting the person in a dream that night. When you first do this, you may wake up from a dream and remember that you have visited the person in the dream state. This is good, but you should keep practicing until you are lucid in the dream while you are visiting the person. Go back into the dream, first repeating your intention to visit that person in that time and that place. Then, spin your whole dream body in a standing position with your arms outstretched, so that you can vividly feel your body in motion. This same spinning technique helps when you are in a lucid dream and feel yourself starting to wake. To avoid waking, begin spinning, and repeat your target phrase over and over again. Notice when you are spinning if you are moving clockwise or counterclockwise. A counterclockwise spin tends to get you out of the body quickly, while conscious; a clockwise spin tends to send you deeply into sleep, but also takes you out of the body.

Step 4: Creative Dreaming

This involves solving a problem in the lucid dream state. Before bed, decide on a problem you need to solve. Frame your problem in your mind as a question. Once you have selected the 'problem question,' write it down and also memorize it. When you are doing the lucid dream exercises here, remember your question and see yourself looking for the answer in your next lucid dream.

Now, here's an exercise for astral travel that is extremely effective, especially if you can direct yourself through it silently. Read it through to yourself, memorize as much of the technique as you can, and then do it on your own. It is most effective that way. Some of you reading this have made tapes for yourself of the other exercises in this book, which worked very well for you. However, the astral traveling exercise does not lend itself to this method because hearing your voice in the physical world will tend to hold you to the physical body as well. You can try it that way, but for most people this interference is too strong to overcome easily. As you will notice, astral travel can be a tool to readily access past and future.

Exercise #1: Astral Traveling

Preparation:

Make sure you will be undisturbed for the next half hour or so. Turn off the phones, lock the door, put the dog or cat out, etc. Turn off any music or noisy electronic devices.

Turn off the lights or darken the windows. Initially being in darkness that imitates nighttime sleep conditions will be helpful.

Get your body into a comfortable position. For beginners it is best to be sitting up to help to maintain awareness. Do not lie down unless you have been able to remain awake in other guided visualizations and know you can do so now.

Take three deep, diaphragmatic breaths to ground and center, put all of your cares and concerns in your worry box, then do your 10-point progressive relaxation exercise. I'm repeating it for you here in case you need a reminder. This is the full version because the deeper you can put your physical body into sleep, the easier it is for you to leave it and astral travel.

10-Point Relaxation:

1. Start with your head, neck, and face.

    a. First relax the skin of your scalp and forehead. Wrinkle your forehead and relax it to feel the difference.

    b. Next relax your eyes, eyelids, and the muscles that move your eyes.

    c. Now relax the muscles of your cheeks.

    d. And next relax the muscles surrounding your mouth.

    e. Swallow to release the tension in your throat.

    f. Gently roll your head around on your neck first left, and then right, to release tension there.

    g. Breathe deeply and notice the accumulated relaxation in your head, face, and neck.

2. Now breathe in deeply and slowly, and as you do, breathe the relaxation you feel in your head, face, and neck into your mind and brain. See it in your mind as a soft cloud drifting in to soothe your mind and brain. Continue to inhale gently, letting this soothing relaxed energy bathe your mind, until your mind has fully absorbed the feeling of relaxation. Feel your mind smooth and relax.

3. Now, with your mind, send a wave of relaxation down through your whole body. Start with your neck, then move it through your upper torso, your arms, hands

and fingers, then down through your lower torso into your legs and finally all the way down to your feet and your toes.

4. Now, keep your focus on your feet. With your mind, TELL the muscles, ligaments, and tendons of both feet to RELAX, to LET GO, and to SLEEP. Repeat that command a second time. Focus on the muscles and tendons of both feet and tell them to RELAX, LET GO, and SLEEP.

5. Next, move your mind's focus up to your legs. LOOK at your legs from your thigh all the way to your ankle. With your mind, TELL the muscles, ligaments, and tendons of both legs to RELAX, to LET GO, and to SLEEP. Again, Repeat the command a second time. Say it to yourself as you do.

6. Move your attention to your lower torso. Focus on your abdominal area… in your mind's eye see your intestines, bladder, sex organs, kidneys, and abdominal muscles; with your mind, tell them to RELAX, LET GO, and SLEEP. Repeat that. Tell them again to RELAX, LET GO, and SLEEP.

7. Now bring your attention up to the organs and muscles of your upper torso. Focus your attention on your heart, your lungs, your stomach, liver, gallbladder, spleen, and on your solar plexus and all of the muscles of your chest and upper abdominal area. With your mind, tell them all to RELAX, LET GO, and SLEEP. Again, repeat the command. Tell them again to RELAX, LET GO, and SLEEP.

8. Look now, with your mind, at the muscles of your back… start at the base of the neck and go all the way to the base of the spine. Tell all of these muscles, RELAX, LET GO, and SLEEP. Again, repeat the command… RELAX, LET GO, and SLEEP.

9. Bring your mind to focus now on the muscles, tendons and ligaments of your arms, hands and fingers… with your mind, tell them also to RELAX, LET GO, and SLEEP. Again, repeat the command… RELAX, LET GO, and SLEEP.

10. Now FEEL your entire body, completely relaxed, asleep, while your mind is still and alert. This is the *10-state* where your mind is generating a smooth alpha wave, is totally relaxed yet awake and alert, and your body is asleep. Say to yourself '10,' and be aware you are in this state of mind awake-body asleep. Say it again, '10.' And one more time, '10.'

Magical Workplace and Energy Screen:

• Move in your mind to your workplace on the inner planes. As always, check out your workplace to see what, if anything has changed. Changes in it reflect changes and growth in you and your life.

- Take up your energy screen from your worktable and expand it to form a doorway big enough for you to step through. Look through it to see a long hallway lined with doors to past and future lives. Step through.

- **Part 1:** As you step through hold in your mind the focus that you wish to visit a lifetime in the past that has some important bearing on this current life. Don't let go of that focus.

    A. Allow yourself to feel a sensation of speed as doors on either side of the hall flash by you, faster and faster, and a sensation of spinning as the hall begins to spin around you, becoming more and more of a spinning tunnel that you feel you are speeding through. Don't be surprised if you begin to hear a high-pitched whine (your own energy) or a sound like wind rushing or roaring.

    B. Come to a stop as you are deposited in front of the door you had focused on, to go back to a life that has some bearing on this one.

    C. Look at the door and make a note of any markings or numbers. Walk through it. On the other side, turn and look back at it. Note if it has changed. Put your hand out and feel it. Feel the texture. Bend down and put your hand on the floor beneath your feet. Feel what you are standing on. Look at the space around you. Note if you are indoors or outside and what type of place you are in. Bring your other senses in. How does the air smell? Taste something. Look around for any information that can tell you what year this is, or what type of life you led in this time frame. Look down at yourself. You will see the body you wore in this past life. Is it man, woman, or child? What do you have on your feet? Find a surface that is reflective, and look at yourself in it. Now turn and find the door you came in through right behind you. Move through it, and back into the hallway of doors. You will remember all you have seen.

- **Part 2:** Hold in your mind a second travel destination in the present time frame. For example, focus on visiting a close friend. Again, feel the sensations of speed and spinning. Be sure to hold your friend's face steady in your mind as you see the hallway speeding by and spinning around you to form a tunnel. You come to a stop wherever your friend is.

    A. Look around your friend to see where he (or she) is. Interact with the environment as before. You can get feedback on this later.

    B. Give him a message. You can check back later to see if he received it.

- **Part 3:** Hold in your mind a destination on another planet – for example, Mars. Again, re-enter your hallway or tunnel, hold Mars in your mind, and concentrate on the sensations of speed and spinning. Stop and find yourself standing on the surface of Mars.

A. Look around to see what you see. Interact with the environment. When you come back you can check information about Mars and get feedback.

- **Part 4:** Again hold your mind on a new destination. This time it is the physical room that your body is sitting or lying in. Re-enter your hallway or tunnel, holding the thought steady. Again, use the sensations of speed and spinning to travel through the tunnel. Return to the room your physical body is in.

   A. Stand in front of your body, and look at it. Turn around and sit or lie back into it. Allow yourself to settle in, feeling the re-merging with the physical begin to happen. Just before it is completely joined stand up out of your body. Feel the sense of separation as you do this. It is easier to experiment with getting in and out of the body when your connection between the two is not completely joined. Try this one or two more times. Also, this helps you to overcome the snap-back tendency that occurs when you see your body.

- **Part 5:** Now hold your mind on another destination – the roof. This time since you are moving such a short distance, merely float up through the rooftop, and come to a sitting position on top of the roof.

   A. Look at the rooftop. What is it made of? Feel it. Look around at the surrounding area. When you are done you can get confirmation on all that you see.

- **Part 6:** Hold your mind, focused now on your body, back in the room it is in. Float back down through the rooftop and come to a standing position in front of your body again. Turn and sit or lie back down into it. You may feel a snapping, or return of warmth to your body as you fully settle in.

Return:
Count yourself back to normal waking consciousness from 10 backward to 1. Then you return to 1 you will be fully awake and remember everything you have seen, felt, and done.

End of Chapter Exercises

---

1. Meditate daily.

2. Do a telepathy exercise with a friend and include remote viewing.

3. Practice the astral traveling techniques daily. Maintain a written record of your journeys.

4. Record your dreams. Practice the exercises in the Omni Experiment.

5. Try dream sharing with someone. Set a night for your dream, then before sleep rub your Third Eye and ask your guide to give you a dream together with your partner. Ask to be awakened immediately upon completion of the dream. Write it down, and the next day talk to your partner and compare dreams. He should show common elements.

Here are some examples:

In a dream that I shared with John, he and I each experienced a dream in which we were in school. We had entirely different dreams, each learning something different, but we met in the cafeteria for lunch.

In a dream together that four of my past students had, (one man and three women) the women all dreamed they were hunting some version of a furry animal – and trying to put it in a cage. The young man (he was single) dreamed he was a squirrel in a cage hanging on a wall with three cats trying to get at him. That has always been one of my favorites! Especially since the women never knew that the gentleman in question was gay!

Suggested Reading

- *Journeys Out Of The Body* by Robert Monroe
- *Far Journeys* by Robert Monroe
- *Cosmic Journeys* by Robert Monroe
- *Astral Projection: Llewellyn's Practical Guide* by Denning and Phillips
- *Astral Projection and Psychic Empowerment* by Joe Slate
- *Techniques of Astral Projection* by Douglas Baker
- *Flying Without a Broom* by D.J. Conway
- *The Ultimate Time Machine* by Joseph McMoneagle

Conclusion

Using the Abilities You Have Learned

In Psychic Development Levels 1 and 2 we learned to open and develop our psychic and intuitive abilities, and how to work with energy. In Psychic Development Level 3 we went beyond that to learn to work with various divinatory tools and more developmental tools. And now you find yourself armed with ability and knowledge and wondering where to go with it.

The real purpose of these three psychic development courses of study is, and always was, self-improvement. They are intended to help you to enrich your life, to make it better in every way.

Those of you who have completed all three levels should not just find your psychic/intuitive abilities working better than ever before, you should feel better, physically and emotionally, be more centered and grounded, and have a real focus on where your life is going and where you want it to go. Psychic development is first and foremost for you.

Many of you will be content with that, and with using the divinatory tools you learned in this book for yourself and your family. Those of you who want to develop this ability well enough to become a professional psychic need to continue practicing on as many 'guinea pigs' as you can find, until you feel secure and comfortable with all of the areas we have covered.

And if you do work toward becoming a professional, always remember this: Although you certainly can accept money for your services (check the laws in your state... some states require a license to practice professionally), it is not about money. It is always about using the gifts you have developed for the highest good of the person for which you are reading. It is not about you, or your ego, about being the best, or about what someone thinks of you. It is about your client, the person who has come to you for a psychic reading and advice. The best psychics are totally selfless while they are reading. That is why they can accurately access issues in a clients' lives without personal bias.

Those of you who desire to be future-oriented psychics now have enough of a background to start reading in earnest. Those of you who want to add Tarot or another divinatory system to your repertoire should begin studying the method of your choice right away. You will find that your studies here have given you a great edge in learning these divinatory methods. Those of you who want to become channels or mediums need to continue your studies as well.

I often tell people that all mediums are channels first, just as all channels are psychics first. Each builds upon the next, much as a brain surgeon must first be a surgeon and a doctor. Each specialty is built upon the foundation of the first.

Many of you who studied these pages, and also Psychic Development Levels 1 and 2, are eager to plunge into mediumship NOW. That would be a grave error. You do not have the necessary tools, ability, or protection yet. Relative to channeling and mediumship you are still a beginner, and entry into that field without proper training can be very dangerous since it leaves you so very open to invasion of all sorts. If you do decide to go on to become a channel, a medium, or both, you need to continue your studies, building on what you have learned here. The Anastasi System Levels 4, 5, and 6 are available in both book form and on CD. I also highly recommend finding an instructor to study with in person for these higher levels of development. You may locate a reputable instructor both on www.AnastasiSystem.com and www.InfiniteQuest.com.

To conclude your studies here, I've included two more exercises. You should renew your cone of power, along with your 1-Month and 1-Year Programming. These exercises were part of Psychic Development Levels 1 and 2. You should also repeat your Psychic Development Aptitude Exercise (see Chapter 1) and compare it to your previous ones to see how much you've improved.

Exercise #1: 1-Month Programming Using Self-hypnosis

1. Take three deep breaths as you ground and center yourself.

2. Put yourself in the white light.

3. Do your 10-Point progressive relaxation.

4. Move to your magical workplace, and put your cares and concerns into the worry box outside the door. Go inside.

5. Turn 360 degrees around and see what has changed or been added since you were last here. Make a mental note of it.

6. Move now to your worktable, and turn on the energy screen there.

7. Now you will do your 1-Month Programming.

    a. See yourself on the screen, looking exactly the way you did this morning in your mirror. Now, think about how you want to look physically. Project that image over the first until the first image is gone and only the second remains.

Say to yourself, "This is how I will look within one month from now." As you watch, let the image float off the screen and drift off into the universe, where it will be able to manifest physically within the next month.

b. Again, see yourself on the screen as you are now, and think about how you want to feel health-wise in the next month. Now see a vibrant, radiant, smiling and totally healthy YOU superimpose its image over the first you on the screen. Say to yourself, "This is how I will feel physically within one month from now." Float that image off the screen, too, and send it off into the universe so it can manifest in your life.

c. Look at the blank screen again, and again let an image of the current you appear on the screen. Project an image of self that is smiling, happy and joyous onto the screen until it is superimposed over the first you. Say to yourself, "This is how I will feel emotionally within one month from now." Once again, float the image off the screen and watch it move out into the universe. Let it go.

d. Now look again at the blank screen. See yourself again; as you are now, but this time see yourself completing something you have wanted to get done. You see yourself put the last touches on the job, smiling, while you feel a sense of happy satisfaction. Say to yourself, "I will finish this job within one month from now." Float that image off the screen and let it go, too, as it moves out into the universe.

e. Last, look at your blank screen and see again an image of the current you there. See yourself doing that particular psychic thing that you want most to be very good at. See yourself successful. Feel the happiness of doing something well. Now, float this image off the screen, too, and let it go out into the universe.

8. Now turn off your energy screen, and step back from your worktable. Turn around 360 degrees again in order to see what, if anything, has changed in your workplace. When you are done move out of your workplace and count yourself back from 10 to 1, normal waking consciousness.

9. It is a good idea to do your programming monthly, and also annually. You can also do it in-between if there is something special you want to program!

Programming Your Cone of Power

Here is a combination exercise that uses the Chakra Exercise to open the *cone of power*.

1. Ground and center yourself. Take three deep diaphragmatic breaths and feel your whole body settling deeply into your chair. Feel any tension ground into the floor.

2. Visualize your worry box, and put into it all of your present concerns.

3. Use your 10-point relaxation technique to calm your body.

4. Focus on the center of your chest, and see a point of white light there. Let the white light grow and expand until it fills all parts of your body and joins with the white light in the aura around you.

5. Visualize a light source above you pouring brilliant white light energy into your aura.

6. Pull white light into your Root Center while you breathe in, and see it turn red as it enters and activates the Root Chakra. Watch the chakra begin to spin.

7. When the Root Center feels full let the red light spin up your spine to the Sacral Center. Let it enter the Sacral Center as at the same time you draw in white light from the aura around you with a breath. See the two light sources merge into the orange light of the Sacral Center.

8. When that center feels full let the orange light spin up your spine to the Solar Plexus Center. Let it enter that center. At the same time, draw in white light from your aura with your breath. See the two lights merge in the Solar Plexus Center as a brilliant yellow light.

9. Again, when that center feels full let the yellow light from it spin upward into the Heart Center, and draw white light from your aura into your heart at the same time. Watch the two light sources merge into a green light in your chest.

10. When the Heart Center feels full let the green light from it spin up into your Throat Center, and at the same time breathe white light in from your aura. Watch the two merge into a blue light in your Throat Center.

11. When the Throat Center is full let the blue light from it spin up into your Third Eye Center. Breathe in white light from your aura, and see the two lights merge into a deep indigo in the Third Eye Center.

12. When it feels full let the indigo light spin upward into your Crown Center and breathe in white light from your aura. See the two merge into the violet light of the Crown Center.

13. Now, in your mind's eye, reach down to your Root Center, and gather the red light energy there. Bring it up, spinning to the Sacral Center, and add the orange light from it. Bring both up, spinning to the Solar Plexus Center and add the yellow light from it. Bring all three up, and add the green light of the Heart Center into the mix. Spin all four up to your Throat Center and add in the blue light from

it. Keep them spinning together as you pull them all up into your Third Eye Center, adding indigo, and finally up to your Crown Center, adding violet.

14. Now, let all of that spinning rainbow of color flow out the top of your head as you exhale, and breathe the rainbow of colors into a purple spinning ball floating over your head. As the rainbow of colors enters, the ball spins faster and faster, sharpening on one end to form a cone. This is your *cone of power*. It is your 8th Chakra that you have now brought to conscious awareness. If you put your hands up over your head, you will feel it there, like an almost-solid cushiony cone above your head. It will be visible to clairvoyants.

15. Now to activate it, you need to program it. First, in your mind's eye, take a tendril of green light from your Heart Center and direct it up into the cone. Next, take a tendril of blue light from your throat and direct it upward into the cone. And last, take a tendril of indigo light from your Third Eye and direct it up into the cone. Each time, say to yourself, "Cone of power, 8th Chakra, help me to develop powers of clairvoyance. Be an observer to let me know if I am ever in any danger, physically, mentally, emotionally, or psychically."

16. When you are done, mentally cut the tendrils of energy entering the cone from each of the lower centers, and then send all of the energy out the top of the cone and back into the universe. The cone of power, or 8th Chakra, will remain active in your aura, and will grow in power over time the more you use it. Remember, when you recognize it working in your life, follow its guidance… that will reinforce it and it will grow. Ignore it, and it will gradually atrophy and its power diminish.

About the Author

Like many who realize their psychic gifts later in life, Sandy Anastasi awakened to her abilities in her late 20's. She understood that many people develop deep psychological problems because their psychic abilities are misunderstood and often blocked. These insights and an inner need to pass on her knowledge and abilities led her to begin teaching others to develop their own psychic gifts. She believes that if you are psychic, you MUST use your gifts, or at least learn to control them, or they will use you!

Sandy has many psychic gifts, but she believes her greatest to be the ability to identify and emulate the gifts of others. Because of that she is uniquely suited to teach people to open and develop those very gifts in themselves.

Sandy has been a professional psychic and astrologer since 1979. She holds a B.S. degree from Adelphi University and has teaching certifications in several fields. In addition to teaching, Sandy has worked as a Safety Engineer, and owned her own small book store for many years before retiring to become a full time psychic counselor, writer and teacher. Sandy's writings include books on Astrology, Kabbala, and Tarot, as well as Psychic Development.

Sandy has also appeared on many radio and television shows over the years, most notably *Crossing Over* and *Cross Country* – both television shows hosted by her good friend and former student, John Edward. She currently lives in Florida with her husband and four dogs.

Additional Products and Services

If you enjoyed this book, you may be interested in the many other products and services offered at www.SandyAnastasi.com.

Personal Readings With Sandy Anastasi

Are you interested in communicating with your Guides and Higher Self in order to obtain key messages that can help you overcome the challenges you will be facing in the future? Or would you like to revisit and learn important lessons from past lives you may have lived? Are you interested in finding out just how astrologically compatible you are with your friends, family, and significant others?

The benefits of having these insights are HUGE. Many people can live for decades without having access to such information, which can provide a critical insight in how to move on and move up in life. And there are many options to fit your specific needs, such as:

- Channeled Readings
- Past Life Reading Using Tarot and/or Astrology
- Death and Afterlife Charts
- Astrology
- Astrology Comparisons

For a limited time only, I am still willing, able, and excited to take on new clients. However, I can only handle so many one-on-one sessions in a given week and I'll always give scheduling preference to my loyal client base. So if you're interested, please book as soon as possible in order to get your spot! Rates and additional information can be found at www.SandyAnastasi.com.

Workshops and Classes

Many of my clients find that the workshop environment is an ideal way to make large gains in their skills and understanding of these topics. And I agree, because workshops provide many benefits and opportunities that cannot be wholly replicated in book format. These advantages include:

- In class demonstrations for hands-on experience.

- Immediate feedback from myself and other skilled instructors.
- The ability to meet with other highly motivated people that are interested in this area of learning and development.
- Question and answer sessions for those burning questions on your mind.
- An environment full of high energy from the instructors and other students.
- An affordable cost compared to one-on-one training.

For a current listing of available workshops, please visit www.SandyAnastasi.com.

Appearances, Interviews, & Lectures

I also am available for appearances, interviews, and lectures outside of the classes and workshops already listed. Please inquire for availability, topics, and (if applicable for the particular format) pricing.

Books & Audio CDs

If you're like a majority of my friends, colleagues, and clients, then I know that an interest in one genre will turn into an eager desire to explore them all... and that's a good thing! Often some your biggest insights and "ah ha" moments will come in areas you least expect it. So while your primary interest may be in spiritual channeling, experience in tarot reading may be the key to unlocking your ability (or at least guiding you into the right direction).

In terms of topics, my 30+ years of experience and training has allowed me to create over 100+ books and CD sets covering the following:

- Crystal and Stones
- Divination
- Dowsing
- Energy Healing
- Healing
- Kabbala
- Meditation
- Numerology

- Philosophy

- Psychic Development

- Psychic Protection

- Channeling and Spirit Communication

- Radionics

- Tarot

So regardless of which genre you're on now, there is something for everybody and something to expand into to diversify your skills and talents.

Most Popular Products

- The Psychic Development Series (books and CDs). This six-part series will systematically teach you drills and techniques that will greatly improve your current psychic abilities, regardless of your current skill level. Topics covered include: energy balancing, how to send and receive information, remote viewing, radionics, channeling/mediumship, soul retrieval, and much more!

- Basic Tarot (books and CDs). Using the Rider Waite deck—The meanings of all the cards are discussed as well as their history and many uses. Students may use any deck utilizing 78 cards. The basic Celtic cross layout is used while finishing with students doing simple but accurate readings

- The Astrology Series (books and CDs). This series will teach you the many components of reading, creating, and interpreting astrological charts. Part 1 begins with learning the basic meanings of the symbols, planets, and houses while the advanced levels cover the nuances of lunar nodes, interceptions, decans, and other important topics that are often ignored or misunderstood.

- The Psychic Development Workshops (transcripts and CDs). These expand upon the book series listed above, particularly in the following topics: psychic self-defense, seeing and feeling the aura, using the pendulum, astral travel, crystal gazing, and psychometry.

- Kabbala Pathworking (books and CDs). A unique experience in exploring the 22 paths of the Kabbala; an ancient system that becomes a roadmap to delineating the soul path to enlightenment. A series of guided visualizations on each Path are designed to open the doors of your unconscious to the energies of the Higher Self and the God consciousness within.

Free Support Materials

In order to help you get the most out of the content of the books and tapes, many of the exercise sheets and other support materials are freely available for download online at www.SandyAnastasi.com (For example the crown Chakra mandala and the Psychic Development Aptitude Test). There you will also find free gifts and bonuses, such as a downloadable Chakra meditation audio that you can use to balance your body's energy system. You are allowed (and highly encouraged) to give and distribute these materials in whatever ethical manner you deem appropriate to others that have an interest in this type of journey.

LaVergne, TN USA
27 January 2011
214217LV00001B/110/P

9 780578 030418